To my darling wife, Rosalie,
in acknowledgement of her
constant love.

Eli S. LeJeune

THE STORY OF HUMANKIND

REVIEW COPY
Not For Resale

AUSTIN MACAULEY PUBLISHERS™
LONDON • CAMBRIDGE • NEW YORK • SHARJAH

A CIP catalogue record for this title is available from the British Library.

ISBN 978-1-78693-399-7 (Paperback)
ISBN 978-1-78693-400-0 (E-Book)
www.austinmacauley.com

First Published (2017)
Austin Macauley Publishers Ltd.
25 Canada Square
Canary Wharf
London
E14 5LQ

CONTENTS

THE STORY OF HUMANKIND

This is a comprehensive up-to-date survey of the scientific accounts of the creation of the Universe, the physical origins and evolution of mankind, and the continuous search for spiritual fulfilment.

This book sets out, in a clear and jargon-free way, the most up-to-date scientific discoveries concerning the creation of the Universe and the physical origins of life on planet Earth. The author conveys the wonder and mystery of the process by which a few small bundles of self-replicating cells have evolved, over billions of years, into all forms of life, including *Homo sapiens.*

Other topics covered are: What is the explanation for the existence of suffering and evil? What is morality, what is free will and what is the impact of spirituality and religion on our lives today?

The author has made extensive researches into natural history and anthropology and has lectured to several inter-faith groups. Drawing on his studies in the development of ethics and the history of religious ideas, he sheds new light on the above fundamentally important topics.

He provides an analysis of the interface between scientific precepts and religious faith, while highlighting the areas of disagreement. The author has prepared a very useful explanation of the various relevant scientific terms used.

The book should appeal equally to people who come either from a scientific or a religious background. Even those who do not profess any particular religious attachment, but are prepared to be challenged intellectually, will be sure to find plenty to satisfy their curiosity.

About the Author

After graduating from Sheffield University, Eli S. LeJeune worked for several years in a financial and commercial environment, both in Britain and abroad, before devoting his time to extensive anthropological research.

Eli is married to Rosalie and they have three daughters.

INTRODUCTION

"Basically, I have been compelled by curiosity"

Mary Leakey, paleoanthropologist

In February 2009 there was a flurry of media activity in many parts of the world in order to mark the bicentenary of the birth of Charles Darwin. Newspaper articles and television programmes examined every aspect of his life, and there were several investigations into his pioneering scientific findings as well as those of his contemporary, Alfred Russel Wallace.

Many years earlier I had been "compelled by curiosity" to delve into the latest theories concerning natural history and anthropology. But my studies had taken me along a different pathway. While trying to get to grips with the scientific aspects of these vast and fascinating subjects I sought to enrich my understanding by introducing the God dimension.

I had prepared some notes on the subject of the alleged clash between science and religion and these notes grew into talks, which I subsequently gave at five different locations in London and Reading. These lectures, together with the feedback I received from my audiences, have provided the seed-corn which has now grown into this book.

A visit to any library will demonstrate that there are dozens of books which explain, in some detail, the science surrounding the initial creation of the Universe, the laws of gravity, electromagnetism, background radiation, and the events leading to the formation of the galaxies, our sun and the planets. Such books may include an exposition of how, after the initial creation of the Universe, the process of mutation by natural selection has resulted in the evolution and wonderful profusion of life on planet Earth from primitive one-cell bacteria, more than 3.5 billion years ago, to today's sophisticated and dominant *Homo sapiens*. Many of the authors of such books hail from an atheistic or agnostic background and they cannot visualise any role at all for a deity, either in the initial creation event or in the subsequent evolution of vibrant complex life on our planet.

Equally, there are various books and pamphlets, written by many theologians, evangelists and some biologists, whose agenda is the complete denigration of all the scientific theories of creation as well as the Darwinian ideas about the evolution of species. They maintain that the first book of the Hebrew Bible, *BERESHEET* (Genesis), is the unalterable template, literally setting out, for all time, the initial stages of the creation of the Universe, the celestial bodies, the oceans, the continents, the fishes of the sea, the reptiles, the various birds and animals and, finally, Adam and Eve, mankind, all in the space of six days. Many respected religious and lay people all over the world still cling to the belief that this very comprehensive creative activity occurred less than 10,000 years ago and emanated directly from the spoken word of God. Such people usually deny that there has been an intricate process of gradual evolution, stretching back over billions of years.

About two years ago I was delighted to come across a fascinating book, "*The Great Partnership,*" by Rabbi Lord Jonathan Sacks, who retired in 2013 after twenty-two years as the inspirational Chief Rabbi of Great Britain and the Commonwealth. This book, quite apart from the many others he has written, provides a distinctive insight into religious belief and morality, as well as describing the interface between science and religion. More recently I have added two other outstanding volumes to my collection, both dealing with a subject matter similar to the theme of my own book: "*The Language of God,*" by Dr. Francis Collins, an outstanding American scientist, as well as "*Gunning for God,*" by Dr. John Lennox, professor of mathematics at the University of Oxford and a "big hitter" in various public debates against those who nurture a keen desire to abolish all aspects of religious faith.

Most people who believe in a deity want to spread the word that religion and science should not be at daggers drawn. Naturally, we all approach the subject from different perspectives – after all, there are several alternative pathways to get to the top of any hill. In this book I have chosen to describe, in some detail, the fascinating scientific theories relating to the creation of the Universe and the physical origins of all life on planet Earth. The later chapters touch on the God dimension. I set out the widely-held conviction, which has prevailed for thousands of years, that there is, and there has always been, a superhuman Creative Intelligence affecting every aspect of our lives. In addition, I devote separate chapters to other topics: spirituality, religion and morals, the existence of free will, and the question of evil. In the last chapter I make an attempt to anticipate and answer some of the questions commonly raised by unbelievers.

Three or four generations ago thinking men and women were involved in arguing the merits of Communism versus Capitalism, universal suffrage, the power of the Trade Unions, the rise of Nazism, the creation of new nation states in Africa and Asia, the alleviation of poverty and the abolition of slavery. Today we are witnessing a new sport: a frontal attack against religious belief spearheaded by atheists, humanists and several scientists who are vociferous followers of Darwin. During the last two decades some non-believers have metamorphosed into polemicists and evangelists, writing books and giving lectures all over the world in order to deny, in a forceful and unseemly manner, the existence of the one unseen God, while urging us all to embrace their doctrine. Their declared desire is to consign religious faith and practice to the dustbin of history.

All those who have an atheist worldview believe that science has proved them right so far. Some of them are preaching the gospel that God is no more than a "God-of-the-gaps," holding sway over ever-decreasing spheres of life, particularly in areas where science has not yet been able to find a satisfactory explanation of a perceived natural phenomenon. Of course, the atheists are fully entitled to hold on to their beliefs and to propagate them. But, like so many people in many parts of the world, I have been unhappy at the gratuitously offensive language levelled against all forms of religious observance. The vituperation heaped upon the belief and practice of countless millions of people, whose lives have always included a necessary faith component, has gone beyond the bounds of reason, and I characterise the approach of these opinionated men as both misguided and uncivil.

It is axiomatic that members of the human race are both biological and theological beings. Mankind is very much more than a collection of cells and genes enclosed in a bag of flesh and bones, going about our lives in a robotic or mechanistic way. We are endowed with a powerful brain with the capacity to use our talents in all sorts of creative ways, while allowing our imagination to roam over matters outside the "here and now". Crucially, uniquely among all animals, mankind has made constant attempts at grappling with matters of the spirit. We understand the concept of time: we have the capacity to remember the past and plan for the future.

The basic premise of this book is that, while science provides us with a wonderful narrative as to "how" the physical realities came about, we have to rely on spirituality to address the missing "why" of the narrative. The intention is to refute the atheist contention that we live in a purposeless world. I reject the notion that men and women are nothing more than a different species of animal controlled by a large brain with only a modicum of free will.

About 9,000 years ago our nomadic ancestors started constructing permanent villages in order to foster mutual help. But, in Gobekli Tepe, on a hill in the Anatolian region of Turkey, there are clusters of buildings which were constructed some 11,000 years ago which tell a very different story.

They were built not by villagers or farmers who intended to settle and live co-operatively, but by nomads who were constantly on the move. The driving force was religion, not agriculture. It appears that our hunter-gatherer forbears needed a place of reflection, worship and temporary shelter as they made their way across the landscape in search of prey. A similar situation seems to have occurred in Ceibal, in what is now Guatemala. Structures were built, not to reside in, but as a place where people assembled for religious festivals prior to dispersing into the forests to forage and hunt. These two examples tell us that religious worship preceded urban settlement, rather than the other way around as we would expect. Maybe the truth is that collaborative prayer sessions were the precursors to social integration.

Stephen J. Gould has introduced a memorable phrase, *"non-overlapping magisteria,"* while stating the obvious fact that faith and science do not conflict because they occupy different domains of knowledge and experience. Faith and scientific rationality must be treated as complementary disciplines, areas of knowledge and belief to be delved into by all people who seek to conduct their lives in a purposeful, meaningful, rounded and fulfilling way.

Of course, mankind's needs originate primarily in the animal world: the need to seek food, find a mate and defend territory. From time immemorial our peripatetic hunter-gatherer forebears have grappled with fundamental questions of both physical existence and with matters of the spirit. We have an unquenchable desire to understand what is "out there" and to come to terms with the nature of the forces which created the Universe, and which have steered us to our present level of sophistication. People have always been asking searching questions: "How did mankind come to be on planet Earth?" and "How can we best relate to our neighbours and our environment?" Attempting to find satisfying answers to these and other questions in this vein, this is how formal religious practices developed and how we began our ongoing dialogue with the Almighty.

Because I have a keen interest in inter-faith dialogue, I have sketched out, in brief, what I have learnt from observing and studying some of the practices of religions other than my own. Although I am the son of a Rabbi, and a descendant of rabbinical ancestors who have lived for many years in the Kabbalistic town of Tsefat (Safed), the opinions and interpretations I am presenting here are those of myself as a committed layman. I am hoping that this book will be of interest to those who do not necessarily have specialist knowledge of either theology or anthropology.

I am starting from first principles in order to explain the issues as comprehensively as possible without appearing tedious or boring. I suspect that some cosmologists and theologians will find some sections of this book rather mundane. However, I wish to address myself to the many who still have a desire to tackle topics which some might consider controversial.

CHAPTER 1

Creation: The Science

"At this moment it seems as though science will never be able to raise the curtain on the mystery of creation. For the scientist who has lived by his faith in the power of reason, the story ends like a bad dream. He has scaled the mountains of ignorance; he is about to conquer the highest peak; as he pulls himself over the final rock, he is greeted by a band of theologians who have been sitting there for centuries."

Dr. Robert Jastrow, astrophysicist, "God and the Astronomers"

Until comparatively recently most people who bothered to think about the subject accepted the ancient proposition that there had never been an initial creation event and, furthermore, that time had no beginning. The classical Greek view was that the Universe had always existed. According to the Greek philosopher Empedocles, matter was deemed to be eternal and the cosmos was made up of just four elements – earth, water, fire and air. It was not until four centuries ago that scientists were able to come up with a coherent alternative to the Aristotelian conception of the eternal Universe.

This chapter is devoted to describing, in some detail, what the scientists have found out about the initial creation of the Universe and its immediate aftermath. My research has demonstrated that no scientist of any calibre has yet been able to describe, with any degree of conviction, the cosmic conditions existing trillionths of a second *before* creation, although in recent years there have been several references to a scientific proposition which states that, rather than one Universe, there has always existed an infinite series of Multiverses, i.e. the belief that there are parallel universes existing side-by-side in an ever-expanding cosmos. I make reference to some of these theories at the end of this chapter.

In the seventeenth century Johannes Kepler and Isaac Newton began to flesh out a scientific theory of a finite Universe which began at a particular historical moment. Less than 100 years ago Alexander Friedmann and Georges Lemaître put forward some mathematical calculations which suggested that, *ex nihilo* (from nothing), there was an act of creation which occurred approximately 13.8 billion years ago. This was the result of a massive, cataclysmic, explosion, the effects of which have been reverberating through the aeons since then. In fact, the cosmic fluctuations can still be detected today by specialised electronic equipment.

The modern scientific view is that, at the time of creation, all matter and all energy were concentrated in an extremely hot and dense singularity, an infinitesimal microdot. That dot represented the compression of a singular point of infinite density. And then, complying with the law of gravity, a mighty and unprecedented explosion occurred, a "Big Bang" which resulted in matter shooting out, hurtling in all directions. The present cosmologically accepted idea is that, in the first trillionths of a second after creation, time began and the Universe started expanding in size at a phenomenal rate.

Scientists say that, because everything in the Universe is now flying apart at ever-increasing speeds, we could reasonably deduce that, at some fixed point in the distant past, everything – all matter, all galaxies – had originally been bound up together in one incredibly tiny entity.

There is some controversy among the cosmologists and physicists over the actual trigger which sparked off the initial explosion leading to the creation of the Universe, but it is generally agreed that it must have been something outside of time, outside of space and outside of matter. Steven Weinberg, Nobel laureate in physics, explained that, at the moment of creative explosion:

" ... The temperature of the Universe was a hundred thousand million degrees centigrade ... The Universe was filled with light."

The concept of a Big Bang, although generally accepted by scientists today, was the subject of heated disagreement until recent times. In fact, until the 1950's there were two competing scientific theories – Lemaître's idea (that creation occurred at one singular moment) was vying with the "solid state" theory, which was propounded by the leading astronomer at the time, Fred Hoyle. The latter, who believed in the theory of "continuous creation," dismissed the competing theory sarcastically as a Big Bang idea. Hoyle's antipathy to the Big Bang idea was rooted in his complete rejection of the notion of a Biblical deity who created the Universe at a particular moment of history.

Since then the dust seems to have settled on that heated controversy. With some notable exceptions, most scientists have now accepted the idea that the whole Universe was created on a single occasion, in a single cataclysmic explosion, less than 14 billion years ago. The causes of that creative explosion are still shrouded in mystery and the subject remains open for scientific discussion and controversy. In 1951 the Catholic Church gave Lemaître's theory its *imprimatur* – it was deemed free of doctrinal error and it did not contradict the creation story depicted in the Book of Genesis.

This idea of a Big Bang moment of creation was independently confirmed quite accidentally in 1965, when Arno Penzias and Robert Wilson, working at the Bell Laboratories in the USA, detected a mysterious background signal intruding into their electronic equipment. The two scientists were able to conclude that the disturbance was the result of microwave radiation, a kind of afterglow which is present all around us as a consequence of the creative explosion which occurred billions of years previously. This confirmation must have been a source of great pleasure to the ailing Lemaître, who died in 1966.

Lemaître was also among the first scientists to declare that there has been a continuous process of "inflation", which means that the Universe has been expanding ever since it was first created. In 1929 the astronomer Edwin Hubble provided a comprehensive observational foundation for this theory. "Hubble's Law" states that the billions of galaxies in the Universe are continually being pulled apart and propelled in every direction, travelling at velocities proportional to the distance from the Earth and from each other. This phenomenon is not the result of some mysterious force thrusting or pulling the heavenly bodies apart. Rather, it is the consequence of the initial Big Bang explosion.

What was the sequence of events after that cataclysmic explosion? After the lapse of years after Big Bang there was a lowering of the intense temperature, enabling the formation of stable atomic nuclei, in particular hydrogen, helium and deuterium. Much later, the heavier elements such as carbon and oxygen coalesced. Hydrogen and helium were drawn together and, in time, nuclear fusion commenced. Dr. Robert Jastrow, the astrophysicist, when discussing the initial creative explosion, put it this way:

> *"The seed of everything that has happened in the Universe was planted in that first instant; every star, every planet, and every creature in the Universe came into being as a result of events that were set in motion in the moment of the cosmic explosion. It was literally the moment of creation ... The Universe flashed into being and we cannot find out what caused that to happen."*

The scientists say that, about 200 million years after the Big Bang, clumps of matter and clouds of gases began to form and take shape, under the force of gravity. When sufficient clouds of hydrogen, helium and lithium coalesced in one planetary location, stars and galaxies began to form. The temperature inside the stars started to climb to a level high enough for nuclear fusion to begin, thus providing the fuel for them to glow.

For many years scientists have been conducting experiments and theorising about the nature of mass: what is it that holds the subatomic particles in any substance together and stops matter from falling apart and collapsing? Many years ago Peter Higgs, now emeritus Professor of Physics at Edinburgh University, put forward the suggestion that there existed infinitesimally small subatomic particles, things called the Higgs Boson, popularly dubbed the "God particle."

In 2008 the European Organisation for Nuclear Research (CERN) completed the construction of the most sophisticated and costly piece of scientific equipment ever made, known as the Large Hadron Collider. The equipment consists of a

27-kilometre ring of superconducting magnets, located under the Alps in Switzerland. Some 10,000 scientists from 100 countries have been periodically involved in the design of the facility and the running of the equipment in order to test different theories relating to high-energy physics and, in particular, to prove or disprove the existence of the Higgs Boson. Technically, the whole installation complex is known as a particle accelerator, enabling protons to travel almost at the speed of light in order to see what happens when they collide with other protons.

In 2012, they did find evidence of the existence of the elusive Boson and Professor Higgs was duly awarded the Nobel Prize for physics in 2013.

In March 2014 the scientific world was abuzz with reports which further reinforced the theory that inflation has been occurring since Big Bang. An international team of scientists led by Harvard University, working in an observatory at the South Pole, said that they had found gravitational waves which bore the imprint of Big Bang. These waves may tell scientists how the Universe came into existence nearly 14 billion years ago. Albert Einstein had, one hundred years previously, predicted the presence of ripples of energy, but proof of this theory had eluded the scientists until now. The newspaper reports said that scientists described the new finding as "jaw-dropping" and "overwhelming". One of the leading Harvard scientists said that "the implications for this detection stagger the mind. We are measuring a signal that comes from the dawn of time."

Our Sun, Earth and Moon

In order to acquire an elementary conception of the vastness of the cosmos let us consider the following:

1. The diameter of our galaxy alone, The Milky Way, is 100,000 light-years. There are 6 trillion miles (10 trillion kilometres) in one light-year. And there are billions of other galaxies in the Universe.

2. Our sun is just one of billions of stars in our own galaxy, many of which have their own planets orbiting them. This means that there could well be hundreds of millions of Earth-sized celestial bodies in the Milky Way galaxy alone.

3. The diameter of our sun is 1,400,000 kilometres or 870,000 miles. It is big enough to accommodate more than a million Earth-sized planets.

4. The distance from the sun to planet Earth is 150 million kilometres or about 93 million miles.

5. The galaxy closest to our own Milky Way galaxy is called Andromeda and it is 2.5 light-years away.

Scientists say that there is nothing particularly special about our Sun – it is just one of billions of stars in our galaxy, The Milky Way, which, in turn, is just one of billions of galaxies in the Universe. Our solar system had originally consisted of a cloud of stellar dust, part of the debris of the Big Bang. The prevailing force of gravity caused an implosion, an inward collapse of this dust and other Big Bang debris and, say the scientists, this was how our sun was created, about 4.6 billion years ago, i.e. more than 9 billion years after Big Bang. The constant surface temperature of the sun is currently estimated to be in excess of 5,000 degrees centigrade. The sunshine which warms planet Earth is the glow resulting from the continuous process of nuclear fusion, an energy phenomenon which exists in all shining stars, and which is expected to continue for another 5 billion years.

The planets were all formed, millions of years after the sun's formation, by the accretion of the stellar dust and debris from the solar nebula. All the 9 planets in our solar system travel through space at phenomenal speeds, describing huge ellipses round the sun.

Planet Earth, which is the third planet from the sun, hurtles through space at a speed of 107,000 kilometres (67,000 miles) per hour as it orbits round the sun. It is estimated that Earth, the densest planet in our solar system, is 4.54 billion years old and it was created from the remnant of dust left over from the formation of the sun. This planetary dust coalesced, together with the debris of huge quantities of massive boulders which came into existence after Big Bang, thus forming planetoids, small planets. Eventually the mass was large enough to become Earth–sized, and it assumed its present spherical shape under the force of gravity.

Inherent in the initial formation of our planet is the existence of seven or eight huge tectonic plates and several minor ones which are floating on the magma, the molten core of liquid rock and iron bubbling away at a temperature of several thousands of degrees Celsius, located in the centre of the Earth. These tectonic plates, which are about 100 kilometres (60 miles) thick, are constantly shifting and realigning themselves, migrating across our planet at the rate of perhaps 2 or 3 centimetres every year.

In the beginning, planet Earth was a boiling ball of lava (molten rock), and, initially, there was no air around the planet. Around 3.9 billion years ago planet Earth began to be bombarded by meteorites and comets emanating from space. Comets are essentially flying time-capsules dating back to the time when our solar system was formed. Locked inside are pristine examples of the original chemical elements and molecules which were created at the time of Big Bang. These

24

meteorites and comets, carrying crystals laden with water, as well as carbon and amino acids, continued to crash onto the surface of our planet for about 20 million years and, the scientists say, it is these crystals which formed the basis of the raw materials which were vital for the creation of life as we know it. This occurred when, after millions of years, the conditions on planet Earth cooled sufficiently and it became hospitable to living organisms.

Dr. Francis Collins, one of the world's leading molecular biologists and medical geneticists, has said that:

" ... *Nearly all the atoms in your body were once cooked in the nuclear furnace of an ancient supernova ... You are truly made of stardust ..."*

Several millions of years later, the various explosions of magma (the combination of molten rock, iron and other elements which is constantly boiling and fizzing in the centre of our planet) burst forth through the outer crust, thus creating mountains.

Oceans and lakes were created as a result of condensation, augmented by water and ice delivered by comets and asteroids. Today about 70% of the surface of the Earth is covered by water, of which less than 3% is fresh and potable, the rest is saline and ocean-based. The early oceans can be compared to a primordial soup and, the scientists say, it is in this watery environment that, quite accidentally, at odds of trillions to one, life spontaneously emerged for the first time, although nobody is quite sure precisely how this came about.

We know that, in cosmological terms, planet Earth is, indeed, in a truly fortunate and uniquely protected situation. The distance from our planet to the sun is just right to ensure that the prevailing temperature on Earth is neither too hot nor too cold. The tilt of the Earth (23 degrees from the perpendicular) is, once again, just right in relation to the sun, and we are fortunate in being orbited by the moon, which has a huge and important impact on the tides and the fixing of the seasons. Crucially we have a plentiful supply of water and the right gases to sustain life. To complete the explanation why our temperate planet is "just right" in so many ways and why it is popularly named Goldilocks by the scientific community, we should explain that Earth is enveloped by an ozone layer and a magnetic field both of which are crucially important to protect us from most of the life-threatening spectrum of the sun's rays. The Van Allen radiation belt, which girdles the Earth and is held in place by the Earth's magnetic field, is situated 1,000 to 60,000 kilometres above the Earth's surface. Quite uniquely, therefore, everything is just right and is in place to ensure the creation and continuation of complex carbon-based life on our planet.

It is thought that, about 90 million years after the formation of the Earth, the **Moon** came into existence after planet Earth sustained a violent glancing blow from another huge celestial body called Thea, estimated to be the size of Mars. The massive impact which created the moon was highly fortuitous and beneficial for our planet, according to scientists. Not only did it create the moon and enlarge the size of planet Earth, but it enhanced Earth's gravitational pull while ensuring that our planet did not become lifeless like Mars.

Our moon, which is 4.45 billion years old, is a ball of rock 3,500 kilometres in diameter (one quarter the diameter of our planet) and it is the only satellite revolving round planet Earth. The distance from planet Earth to the moon is about 250,000 miles (380,000 kilometres) and its gravitational interaction with Earth is vitally important. It stimulates ocean tides, stabilizes the axial tilt and it gradually slows the rotation of planet Earth round the sun.

If you were to place a telescope in your garden and gaze at the moon on any night of the year you will always see the same craters on the moon surface. This is explained by the fact that the moon makes one revolutionary orbit round planet Earth every 29 days and this coincides with the rotation of the moon on its own axis. This is why the view from Earth is always the same – we do not see the far side of the moon from our planet.

Commencement of Life

Where is the hard evidence for the commencement of life on planet Earth? The first self-replicating molecule is thought to have been created about 3.8 billion years ago and that is now considered by scientists to be the common ancestor of all living things, whether plant or animal. It has been known for some time that graphite located in Western Greenland did contain some signs of extremely primitive life which can be traced back to 3.7 billion years ago.

On 8th November 2013 scientists announced the discovery, in Pilbara, Western Australia, of a fossilised bacterial structure, a "microbial mat" dating back to more than 3.5 billion years. This represents the remains of primitive blue-green algae, which are considered to be the first-ever known form of life as we know it, possessing the important capacity to convert sunlight into food. The process, known as photosynthesis, meant that water could be combined with carbon to form glucose, a simple form of sugar. As a result of that process oxygen was released and the evolution of all living things could begin.

For hundreds of years mankind has been searching for evidence to establish whether or not we are truly alone in the Universe. In spite of the creation of SETI (search for extra-ter-restrial intelligence) numerous theories, probes and, in recent

27

decades, the sending of electronic signals into the stratosphere, there is not one single iota of evidence to indicate that, among all the celestial bodies encircling our sun, there is any other planet which can and does sustain any form of life as we know it.

A summary of the creation timescale appears at the end of this chapter.

Universe or Multiverse?

The word "Universe", of course, implies singularity. However, some prominent scientists working at the Perimeter Institute, a leading Canadian scientific think-tank, as well as at Harvard University and other seats of learning have been studying other ideas.

It would be interesting to make some reference to the following issues which have exercised the minds of various physicists and cosmologists over the past decade or two:

1. What is it that existed just *before* Big Bang and what was the sequence of events which actually triggered the cataclysmic explosion?

2. Is there any evidence to support the idea that, rather than just one Big Bang, there have always been explosions, one after another, entirely due to natural causes, resulting in the creation of a whole constellation of parallel universes?

3. In terms of cosmology what is "nothing" and can we accept the idea that there has always existed a phenomenon, called "Eternal Inflation", which has resulted in the ability of the cosmos to accommodate an infinite number of universes existing side-by-side?

Dr. Param Singh cannot accept the concept of just one Big Bang and prefers to envision a series of explosions, one after the other, which he has called the "Big Bounce," such that, over uncounted trillions of years, an infinite number of universes have been created and subsequently died in a continuous never-ending process.

Another scientist who entertains doubts about Big Bang is Professor Neil Turok. He is inclined to the view that, rather than one Big Bang, there has always been a succession of cyclical creation events, which has meant that the gravitational waves which are all around us today are much weaker than previously thought.

Professor Andrei Linde has been exploring the answer to the question: "what did really happen *before* Big Bang?" He has been promoting the theory that there has always been a scenario of repeated expansion and contraction events, creating a succession of universes. He believes that, if we were to imagine the cosmos as an ever-expanding lump of Swiss Gruyere cheese, then each new universe, when created, moves to occupy one of the holes in the cosmic cheese. He believes that when one universe reaches the end of its natural cycle another universe is automatically created from matter obtained from the pre-existing universe.

Professor Lee Smolin has a similar idea and he refers to the existence of "black holes" which are continuously contracting and expanding, thus creating a never-ending series of new universes existing side-by-side.

Some years ago Professor Stephen Hawking published a landmark book on physics and cosmology entitled "*A Brief History of Time*," in which he wrote:

"The discovery fairly recently of the extreme fine tuning of so many of the laws of nature could lead at least some of us back to the old idea that the grand design (of the universe) is the work of some grand designer."

As he is one of the world's leading atheists, Professor Hawking cannot be expected to entertain the idea that "the grand designer" could be God. Instead, Hawking believes that "spontaneous creation is the reason there is something rather than nothing." He has recently been promoting the idea that, instead of one single Universe (irrespective of how it has been created) it is equally feasible to believe that there exists a constellation of universes created by the natural laws of science. Hawking's theory involves such esoteric concepts as "vibrating strings in eleven dimensions," which even fellow physicists struggle to contend with.

Sir Roger Penrose, the Oxford mathematical physicist, is one of many scientists to take the view that Hawking's recently-minted "M-Theory" does not qualify as "the theory of everything" and it does not have the power to have created the Universe "out of nothing".

In 2014 Professor Brian Cox presented an interesting programme on television in which he embraces the concept of parallel universes. He compared the existence of complex life on our planet with the holding of a lottery. Accepting the possibility of the existence of multiple universes, he said that each universe may have been created spontaneously, and each planet within each galaxy may have each been endowed with unique features from its very inception. He said that, just as each lottery ticket possesses its own unique number, so each planet in each of the multiplicity of universes may possess its own unique characteristics.

Some planets may have no chance of sustaining any form of life because they are travelling in an orbit which is too far from their sun. Others may be too hot or they may be too small or devoid of water or the right gases, or they may be tilted at an angle which is not favourable for the creation of life.

We can postulate, says Professor Cox, that just as there is only one ticket winning the jackpot in any lottery, so planet Earth may have been the only one lucky planet to have been fortuitously endowed with all the right attributes to sustain complex carbon-based life.

Many other scientists, however, have reached the conclusion that all the above theories about the multiverse represent no more than intellectual exercises, speculative philosophical musings and elegant mathematical equations, all designed to degrade the possibility of the existence of the one Creator God. Atheists believe that if people become convinced that our Universe is not unique, and if the idea takes hold that there has never been a singular "Big Bang" moment of creation, this would result in the severe dilution of our long-held belief in the divine message contained in the Bible. It would certainly whittle away the conception of the unique creatorial powers of the Almighty.

One is tempted to ask: "How can speculation surrounding the multiverse idea help us to get a better understanding of the factors which have rendered our planet bio-friendly and fine-tuned for complex life?" I do not think that it gets us any nearer to answering the all-important question: "What was the ultimate origin and purpose of the creation of life on our planet?"

For ease of reference I append below a summary of what the scientists consider to be the timescale of the important cosmological and other early creation events. Some of the terms are explained in later chapters of this book.

APPROXIMATE TIMESCALE IN THE STORY OF CREATION AS REVEALED BY RECENT SCIENTIFIC RESEARCH (BILLIONS OF YEARS AGO)

Big Bang – Creation of the Universe	13.80
Creation of our Sun	4.60
Creation of Planet Earth	4.54
Creation of our Moon	4.45
First Self-replicating Molecules and unicellular microbial life	3.80
Profusion of Prokaryotes, Stromatolites and Primitive Algae	3.60
First Single-Cell Organisms (Archaea, Bacteria)	3.50
First Eukaryotes (organisms with a membrane-bound nucleus)	2.10
Start of Cambrian Explosion	0.54

CHAPTER 2

Evolution: The Science

"Scientists don't have a clue how life began. ... Geologists, chemists, astronomers and biologists are as stumped as ever by the riddle of life."

"Scientific American" magazine, 2011

In the Beginning

As already stated, physicists/cosmologists have worked out that our own planet Earth made its appearance about 4.54 billion years ago, i.e. more than 9 billion years after "Big Bang", and well after our sun made its appearance. At the moment of creation our planet was a boiling mass of primordial hot lava (molten rock). After the surface of the Earth had cooled down, some hundreds of millions of years later, tiny micro-organisms made their appearance, as described in chapter 1. Such is the slowness in the pace of evolutionary change that it took more than 700 million years after the creation of planet Earth for unicellular and microbial life to appear and a further 3.2 billion years before vertebrates and other forms of complex life could get established and start proliferating.

In Shark's Bay, Western Australia, there are stromatolites, biochemical rocklike structures created by a primitive form of algae. These were built in shallow waters and are actually only a few thousand years old but the creators of those structures were similar to organisms which are thought to have existed more than 3.6 billion years ago. They provide vital clues to the initial creation of life. Bacteria and archaea, the first two "kingdoms" of living organisms, can be traced back to more than 3.5 billion years ago.

But it is important to stress that, even today, the scientific community have not yet made their up their minds about the process by which inanimate cells acquired the ability to change spontaneously into creatures with a life force, able to thrive and reproduce. Dr. Francis Collins, who spearheaded the American team which mapped out the human genome about two decades ago, had this to say:

> "How did self-replicating organisms arise in the first place? ... At the present time we simply do not know. No current hypothesis can come close to explaining how the environment that existed on planet Earth gave rise to life."

The scientific world has, up to now, failed to demonstrate how the molecular building blocks of life – proteins – could have been created. No biochemist has been able to produce a living cell in a laboratory.

In 1953 two scientists, Miller and Urey, conducted an experiment in their laboratory in the University of Chicago to try to mimic the wonderful moment, billions of years ago, when life began on planet Earth. They put together hydrogen, carbon monoxide, ammonia, methane and water vapour and subjected the mixture to ultra-violet light and electrical discharges. A few weeks later they detected that several amino acids had indeed been created. This was the first step in the creation of proteins, the building blocks of body tissue. But these were not enough to create life.

You need many more amino acids and, very importantly, you need DNA to combine with proteins and carbohydrates in order to create chromosomes, resulting in the correct coding of the vital genetic information which gets transferred from parent to progeny. In 1953 little was known about the role of DNA in heredity. It has now been ascertained that there needs to be no less than about 200 essential parameters, all working in tandem, in order to create and support life.

There is a consensus among today's scientists that the Miller-Urey experiment cannot be taken seriously because there was a fundamental error in simulating the exact chemical composition of gases that existed in the atmosphere some 4 billion years ago. This is particularly so in relation to oxygen, which represents 21% of the air we breathe, but which may not have been the same when planet Earth was newly created and when it was not fully established in the planetary system.

In 1859 Charles Darwin published his famous book, "On the Origin of Species, or the Preservation of Favoured Races in the Struggle for Life", which introduced the concept of "Mutation by Natural Selection". It appears that the book was in a period of gestation for about 20 years (partly due to his desire not to come out openly against established Church doctrine). His tentative observations were only rushed into print after Darwin had received some notes from another scientist, Alfred Russel Wallace, who had, quite independently, arrived at conclusions similar to his own. Ian Tattersall, in his book "Masters of the Planet", has described the Darwin/Wallace theory as:

"... the preferential survival and reproduction of individuals that are better adapted to their environments than their fellows, in features inherited from their parents ..."

The early tentative ideas, which later developed into Darwin's Theory of Evolution, were first proposed by other scientists just over 200 years ago, and the general principles are now almost universally accepted by the scientific community as well as by many non-scientists (both theist and secular). It must be said, however, that there are still sizeable numbers of people who, being strict adherents of the major religious traditions, are not prepared to deviate from their attachment to a strict literal reading of the Bible, and they have serious reservations about the implications of the Darwinian ideas. For different reasons there are also some scientists who have grave reservations, and they have distanced themselves from the full acceptance of the theory.

Let us be quite clear about Creation and Evolution. Charles Darwin did not attempt to theorise on the nature of the initial creation of the Universe. Until recent times physicists and cosmologists did not speculate on what could have existed *before* Big Bang.

Darwin speculated that just one "primordial form", a simple universal cell, may have been the common ancestor of all living things. His working assumption was that this very first hypothetical common ancestor somehow stirred into life "in some warm little pond". Thereafter, the process of "evolution with modification" took hold. He believed that all species that have ever lived are nothing more than the "lineal descendants" of that first organism. In other words, all life, and all variations on the micro and macro level, they have all resulted from the slight, successive, favourable variations which have taken place in compliance with the principle of "the survival of the fittest."

Darwin's starting point was the evolution of living things, from the self-replicating micro-organisms which evolved some 3.8 billion years ago to the creation of today's *Homo sapiens*. Darwin's book, which incorporates a now-famous sketch, suggests that the process of evolution can be likened to a tree, with all life forms inter-connected.

During the past 160 years Darwin's successors have built up a vast body of scientific knowledge which attempts to provide answers to the most searching evolutionary questions. There has been an exponential increase in our knowledge of the Universe, we have become aware of the marvellous variety of life on Earth, and we have become ever more curious about the provenance of each species.

Darwin's Theory in Brief

Charles Darwin had in mind two stated objectives in his research: to show, firstly, that the various species had not been separately created and, secondly, that natural selection has been the chief agent of change. In his famous book he wrote, "I have called this principle, by which each slight variation, if useful, is preserved, by the term 'natural selection'."

The classic Darwinian belief is that evolution can be compared to a massive tree whose seed was planted just over 3.8 billion years ago. In fact, his book includes a now-famous sketch showing the inter-connectivity of all life we see around us. All life forms, every plant, marine creature, insect, reptile, bird or mammal, we are all ultimately linked to a single ancestor or groups of organisms that sprang to life after the initial creation of the single-cell organisms which were able to self-replicate.

As you cast your eyes over the sturdy trunk, being an imaginary pictorial representation of the evolution process, you observe the growth of numerous mighty branches, here and there. More and more branches become apparent as you go further up the tree. Each branch is sub-divided into ever smaller sub-sub-branches. From each tiny sub-sub-branch you see twigs, some large, others minuscule. The whole tree of life has thousands of branches and countless millions of sub-sub-branches. Each microscopic twig represents one species of life.

Evolution cannot occur if the genetic change manifests itself in only one or two individual animals. Scientists have determined that evolution can only take place and can only become established if the same gene changes occur to a great number of individuals of the same species.

The huge diversity of life which we see around us (bacteria, algae, sponges, fungi, corals, plants, marine creatures, insects, reptiles, birds, and mammals) arises from the fact that the lineages that descend from common ancestors have tended to diverge through aeons of time. So the question is this: what is it that causes this divergence? What is it that causes the minuscule genetic variation between parents and progeny? It is now scientifically established that this departure from the norm is the result of a completely random process, an unplanned mutation in one cell or another. Darwin called it the process of Mutation by Natural Selection. A mutation means that there has been a change in the DNA sequence of a cell's genome. Of course, the concepts of DNA and genome sequencing were completely unknown in Darwin's time.

Some people have formed the impression that the process of evolution takes place in a manner which has no regard to established natural laws. If you were to spill a few drops of ink over 100 pieces of paper you will get 100 different smudges, each one with a tiny variation, depending on such factors as the volume of ink spilt, the tiny difference in the chemical composition of the paper and any variation in the height between the bottle of ink and the paper. In the same way, every step in the evolutionary process is controlled and constrained by the inherent laws of nature. During the process of replication the relevant atoms, molecules, etc. behave exactly in accordance with their own laws. They replicate in accordance with internally established rules.

Proteins attract molecules and grow in a manner dictated by the principle of "survival of the fittest." This applies even with mutations and "rogue genes." The internal workings and procedures may sometimes appear to be strange, merely because mankind has not yet acquired the relevant expertise in understanding their behaviour.

It can be argued that natural selection has no creatorial powers. All that happens is that weaker elements in an organism are removed while the stronger elements are reinforced. That is not creation in the true sense of the word, merely the enhancement of what is already available. Although a beneficial mutation can sometimes take place it is not done consciously. And let us bear in mind that, going back to the origin of life itself, some 3.8 billion years ago, natural selection would have failed had there not been self-replicating genetic material already in existence.

After the successful mating of two parents there could, on occasion, be a copying error in the process of the transmission of genetic material from one generation to the next. There could, in other words, be a cell mutation, a chance event, resulting in the transmission of "rogue" genetic material from parent to progeny. After several tens of thousands of generations this mutation, together with any other mutation which may occur subsequently, may eventually result in subtle but significant variations in physical attributes of the same species or they may, indeed, result in the creation of new species altogether. In biological terms evolution means, briefly, changes in the gene pool. Some genes, inherited from one parent, become more or less numerous than before, resulting in a change in the ratio of the quantity or variety of genes from one generation to the next. This means that certain characteristics of one or other parent do not get passed on to the offspring, thus resulting in a tiny change in the size or colour or some other characteristic feature. Only genes that are strong enough or dominant enough will survive.

The main characteristic of what it means to be classified as a living creature is the possession of living cells. But not all cells are the same. The main divisions are: ARCHAEA, BACTERIA and EUKARYOTES.

Archaea and bacteria are two alternative "kingdoms" of PROKARYOTES, single-cell organisms that lack a membrane-bound nucleus, and they are thought to have first made an appearance about 3.6 billion years ago. By contrast, the more advanced eukaryotic cells do contain a membrane-bound nucleus, and they first made an appearance about 2.1 billion years ago. All cells carry the all-important DNA, which is vital for the purpose of reproduction. The cells of all plants, birds and animals which we can see all around us today are all classified as eukaryotes.

Carl Linnaeus was a Swedish zoologist and physician who lived in the 18th century. He developed the science of taxonomy, the system of classification covering all living things. Originally there were just 2 "kingdoms": Animals and Plants. Today there are 5 main classifications:

(a) ANIMALS (b) PLANTS (c) FUNGI (d) PROTISTS (e.g. slime mould and algae) (e) BACTERIA

In recent years great advances have been made in improving classification procedures. If, for example, we were to compare humankind and tigers we would arrive at the following:

	HOMO SAPIENS	TIGERS
Kingdom	Animalia	Animalia
Phylum	Chordata	Chordata
Class	Mammalia	Mammalia
Order	Primates	Carnivora
Family	Hominidae	Felidae
Genus	Homo	Panthera
Species	Homo Sapiens	Tigris

Two animals can be said to belong to the same species if, upon mating, they can achieve a viable fertile offspring. A bulldog and a poodle both belong to the same species, so a viable offspring can result from their mating. But neither dog belongs to the same species as a gazelle or a sheep so no offspring will result here.

One feature of evolution has attracted considerable attention: nature is surprisingly economical and repetitious. For example, if we were to consider the family of tetrapods (four-limbed creatures) we see various features and attributes which are common to all. Apart from some noteworthy variations, we can observe that they all have two eyes, nostrils, a mouth, lungs and broadly similar digestive and reproductive systems. This is true for mankind, cats, horses, monkeys, bears, etc.

Many beneficial mutations have taken place over the millennia. Dogs have a very highly developed sense of smell. The giraffe has an unusually elongated neck. The ancestors of modern giraffes did have shorter necks, but evolution favoured the animals with longer necks because they were better able to reach the juicier and more abundant food which was found high above ground. A chance mutation must have occurred at some time, such that the animals with longer necks were better able to help themselves to more abundant food, leading to enhanced fitness, better survival rates and a better rate of reproduction.

41

These beneficial mutations have occurred at the biochemical level, but that is not the same as evolution from one species to another.

Scientists say that *Homo sapiens* have experienced a whole series of crucial adaptations, skeletal and muscular, associated with bipedal locomotion. For example, our feet and ankles have lost the flexibility and agility which is important to branch-grasping and tree-hopping apes. Our thumbs have become somewhat elongated, our four other digits have shrunk, relative to those of apes, and our legs have become longer relative to our arms. There has been a significant reduction in the size of our canine teeth and there has been a descent of our larynx and hyoid bone.

For over 3.8 billion years the evolutionary process has enabled live organisms to mutate very gradually from one species to another, achieving ever-higher degrees of adaptation and specialisation, until we reach our present status of *Homo sapiens*. Biologists and geneticists are adamant in their belief that, if you could rewind the evolutionary clock far back, to about 500 or more million years ago, the direct ancestors of mankind would be found to have been a primitive fish or even a bacterium. It must be admitted that, for some people, this is a counter-intuitive or even a shocking idea, but scientists assure us that this is what has really happened.

The late Ha'Rav Lord Jakobovits, who was the distinguished British and Commonwealth Chief Rabbi until 1991, has written a *Companion to the High Holiday Prayer Book*, in which he says:

"... The emergence of man out of lower forms of life need not be disputed. What matters is that man, whatever his physical origin, is a unique creature endowed with intellectual and moral capacity not shared by any other form of life."

42

Darwin's theory emphasises the element of pure luck, i.e. the process of evolution does not involve planning or coercion by anybody. The other important feature is the ability of cells as well as all living creatures to survive in an ever-changing competitive environment – hence the well-known concept of "survival of the fittest." The implication is that all living things, including mankind, are helpless pawns, the victims of their genes. Scientists maintain that evolution is a continuous process which has no goals and no long-term plans except the survival of the fittest organisms. This view is, obviously, contradicted by theologians.

Fossils

In November 2013, in a Sussex auction house, the auctioneer's gavel came down signifying the sale of a fossil, the remains of a *diplodocus*, a rare and sculpturally impressive 17-metre (60 ft.) long dinosaur. An undisclosed institution was prepared to part with more than £400,000 (half a million dollars) for the privilege of owning "Misty", one of only 6 relatively complete diplodocus fossils in the world. Estimated to be about 150 million years old, she had roamed the earth during the Jurassic period in what is now Wyoming, USA.

Many scientific institutions throughout the world, such as the Smithsonian in Washington and the Natural History Museum in London, are proud to display huge life-size dinosaur fossils in their entrance halls or specially designed chambers. It is true that, sometimes, what the public are able to see are carefully moulded plastic or resin replicas, the originals of which are either owned by other institutions or the originals could not be put on display because they are too fragile and incomplete. But, whether original or fake, fossils remain a source of wonder and intense fascination for all visitors.

Fossils are evidence of ancient life-forms which have been preserved by natural processes. They can be found in a variety of locations such as sedimentary rocks, permafrost, amber and tar pits. The process of fossilisation is hastened in places where there is little oxygen, such as the bottom of the sea or in swamps. The term fossil refers to the remains of long-dead creatures and organisms, animal and vegetable, which assume the shape and contours of the former, more solid, parts. It takes a long time to create a fossil, but the skeleton can only be successfully fossilized if it is rapidly buried.

After the death of a prehistoric animal or plant, millions of years ago, its original soft tissue may have been scavenged or naturally decayed. However, its hard parts (skeleton, skull, teeth and shells, even surrounding plant material) may soon become covered by tons of mud, rocks, sand or ice. In time the layers of earth round the skeleton would become hard and compacted.

Assuming the temperature and other conditions are right, the ground water will, in the course of time, dissolve the original skeleton, teeth, etc. After the original bony minerals and excess water are flushed out, a cavity would remain – in effect, the cavity can be likened to a mould which has acquired the shape of the original skeleton. The earth's minerals (e.g. quartz, clay, iron oxides, potash, gypsum, basalt, bauxite and calcite) would then seep into the empty mould and, in time, they would solidify. Put simply, therefore, a fossil is a remineralised copy of the original skeleton and, in that state, can last virtually forever.

The dating of fossils is carried out using carbon-14 isotopes on the sedimentary rocks. The breakdown of radioactive isotopes takes place at a known rate, so the age of the rock in which the fossil is embedded can be calculated. At the end of this chapter I make reference to the phenomenon known as the Cambrian Explosion, when the quantity and diversity of the fossil record increased very rapidly, an occurrence which scientists are not yet able to explain satisfactorily.

When considering the subject of fossils one perennial nagging question arises: have any fossils been found which lend visible and conclusive credence to Darwin's theory of gradual mutation or evolution which, apparently, has been occurring over a long period of time? In other words, have any fossils been found which exhibit "intermediate" features, i.e., features pertaining partly to one species and partly to another? Well, it must be said that, in spite of all the digging and delving all over the world, very few (if any) fossils has been found which directly and conclusively support Darwin's findings.

Some years ago the late Dr. Colin Patterson, who was the senior palaeontologist at the British Museum of Natural Science, ruffled several scientific feathers when he wrote:

"... there are no transitional fossils ... there is not one single fossil for which one could make a water-tight argument ..."

On another occasion Dr. Patterson was quoted as saying, in relation to *archaeopteryx*, that he could not be sure whether it was the ancestor of all birds – which was the view held by several scientists. He wrote:

"Fossils may tell us many things, but one thing they can never disclose is whether they were ancestors of anything else."

Dr. Patterson's views were supported by the late Stephen J. Gould, professor of palaeontology at Harvard, but in recent years there have been several attempts to "explain" or partially amend what he was reported to have said originally. The fact remains, though, that over the past several hundred years scientists everywhere have been able to discover fossils of thousands of species, most of which are now extinct (e.g. mammoths or sabre-toothed tigers). But each is the fossil of one particular species only. Darwin knew this and he was certainly worried that the paucity of fossils of the so-called "intermediate species" would undermine the credibility of his scientific research.

Naturally, there has been a continuous intensive search all over the world for the most important so-called "missing link", i.e., conclusive proof that mankind is "descended from apes". In 1912 there was a buzz in the scientific world over the finding of "Piltdown Man". A skull was produced which consisted of a human cranium with the jaw-bone more typical of an orangutan. Forty years later it was exposed as a fake – it was nothing more than an elaborate fraud perpetrated by an obscure solicitor in Sussex.

In 1861 a fossil hunter in Bavaria, Germany, found the remains of an unusual bird-like creature, the size of a modern pigeon, which we now know as *archaeopteryx*. Some scientists believe that it is a supreme example of the link between a feathered dinosaur and a modern bird. Although exhibiting feathers, these were apparently meant for gliding rather than for active flying. When alive it weighed about one kilo (just over two pounds), it had a bird-like beak and teeth but it had a bony tail like a dinosaur. This creature, which has been dated to about 150 million years ago, has remained a puzzle to palaeontologists, who cannot decide whether it should be classified as a bird or a dinosaur.

Set against the above story is the case of an interesting and ancient fish known as a *coelacanth*. It was originally thought that, in the Indian Ocean between South Africa and India, there existed this rather unusual fish, which had first appeared about 400 million years ago but which was thought to have become extinct some 60 million years ago. In 1938, however, a fisherman

46

in South Africa found a coelacanth in his catch. It appeared to have two appendages, which resembled front paws, and it was thought that this plump sea creature, about one metre long, was an intermediate species, a vital missing link between a fish and some sort of land animal. Since then, further specimens of the same fish have come to light.

Other examples of an apparent stasis in the evolutionary process of species include sponges, horse-shoe crabs and sea cucumbers, all of which have apparently not evolved at all over a period of several hundred million years.

The question which has intrigued scientists is this: what is it that has prevented the normal evolutionary laws to apply to those creatures which have managed to remain unchanged for so long? The scientists can only provide a rather lame explanation for the apparent stasis in these creatures' evolutionary development. They say that perhaps environmental factors may have caused the coelacanth to exist quite happily, apparently undisturbed by predators, for hundreds of millions of years, without the need to comply with Darwinian evolutionary laws. Another theory is that the flesh of the coelacanth has an unpleasant and rather oily taste and this may have deterred potential predators.

Fossil Fuels

No discussion of fossils can be complete without highlighting the importance of fossil fuels in our present civilisation. This term encapsulates coal, petroleum and gas products, extracted from mines, wells, pits, shafts and excavations all over the world. As explained in the next chapter, there was a period of about 60 million years, from 350 to 290 million years ago, which, in geological terms, is known as the Carboniferous Period. This is the time when there was a sustained decomposition and burial of microscopic sea organisms, such as planktons, and there was a hastening in the fossilisation of the remains of the huge volume of dead trees and plants. The remains of unicellular organisms, trapped in sedimentary rocks beneath the sea, became the source of the crude oil and gas products which we use today, while the massive forests and dead woodlands began to be converted into coal deposits.

Although at first glance it would appear that this natural bonanza, which we have been able to extract from the bowels of the earth for many years, is vital for the continued economic progress of mankind, the reverse side of the coin is that we run the risk of despoiling our own atmosphere and ruining our health because of the continuous belching forth of potentially lethal greenhouse gases, such as carbon dioxide, an inevitable by-product of burning fossil fuels. There has been a puncturing of the ozone layer protecting our planet, and this may have been responsible for the increase in skin cancers.

Before the 18th century mankind used windmills and watermills to power whatever simple mechanical and engineering equipment came into use, although the use of coal as a fuel was known in prehistoric times. It is quite conceivable that the Industrial Revolution would not have occurred in quite the same way had it not been for the great advances in technology powered by fossil fuels.

In Britain we rely on coal and gas for the generation of about two-thirds of all our electricity needs. However, experts from the United Nations have repeatedly warned all industrialised countries of the long-term deleterious effects of burning fossil fuels. There are dire predictions of a general rise in global temperatures if we do not reduce or even eliminate our dependence on these fuels without incorporating a reliable technology for the capture and disposal of carbon dioxide.

It must be said that the questions of "global warming" and "carbon footprints" are subjects replete with controversy and they have been the cause of some friction between advanced industrial nations on the one hand and third world economies on the other. In any event, the technical problems inherent in the development of renewable sources of energy (solar, nuclear, bio-ethanol, wind turbines, tides) still need to be addressed.

It is certainly the case that either the relevant technology is in need of substantial improvement or the costs are too high or there are obvious environmental issues to be addressed. As regards the nuclear option there is considerable debate regarding operational safety and the disposal of spent fuel rods. As a result, the so-called "renewable" sources of energy cannot yet be considered to be completely satisfactory substitutes for fossil fuels.

The Cambrian Explosion

An unusual phenomenon occurred during the period of 40 million years from 540 to 500 million years ago which, for reasons which are not fully understood, resulted in an unprecedented abundance and variety in the fossil record. During a relatively short period, known as the Cambrian Explosion, something happened which caused the unexplained abundance of the fossils of many small creatures with no known antecedents – in other words, many ecological niches opened up relatively suddenly.

The fossil record indicates that, up to that time, most living organisms had been relatively simple, single-celled creatures. It is possible, of course, that there had existed much larger organisms of greater complexity prior to that time, but we are left with no fossil record to prove that. Quite suddenly, however, it

49

appears that there was a perceptible quickening in the number and diversity of vertebrates, indicating a rapid acceleration in the evolutionary process. In particular, there occurred an unparalleled ecological complexity among marine animals.

Of course Charles Darwin and others knew about the Cambrian Explosion and, in fact, he thought that this unusual biological phenomenon could be the biggest blow to the acceptance of his theory. He was, after all, promoting the idea that the process of mutation by natural selection was a much gentler process and he was indicating that, normally, the diversification of animal species manifested itself through a much greater number of generations, over dozens of millions of years.

The late Stephen J. Gould, one of the leading scientists and promoters of evolutionary ideas, questioned this apparent glitch in the smooth evolutionary process but he could not account for the remarkable diversity which became apparent during the Cambrian Explosion. It could be, of course, that the increase in the number and variety of animal species was the result of a significant change in climatic and other environmental conditions that had facilitated the fossilization of species which had actually existed for aeons. In the opinion of Gould there could, on the other hand, be a phenomenon in nature, known as "Punctuated Equilibrium" – a long interval of near-stasis punctuated by periods of rapid evolutionary activity.

In the next chapter an attempt will be made to trace the trajectory of the evolutionary process which has taken place during the various geological time-periods.

CHAPTER 3

Evolution: The Last 540 Million Years

"To suppose that the eye, with all its inimitable contrivances for adjusting the focus to different distances, for admitting different amounts of light and for the correction of spherical and chromatic observation could have been formed by Natural Selection seems, I confess, absurd in the highest degree."

Charles Darwin, "On the Origin of Species"

Before taking the story of evolution any further it would be useful to say something about the general scientific ferment which has been the dominant feature of our lives during the last five hundred years, a process which, indeed, is gathering pace every day. Up to the 1500's scientific investigation was not encouraged, and, of course, there were no sophisticated laboratory facilities attached to either commercial enterprises or Church-sponsored seats of learning. In fact, there were attempts at forbidding the publication of books and pamphlets on any subject without the specific approval of the ecclesiastical authorities. In the 17th century a Dominican friar, echoing the thoughts of many people in authority, was quoted as saying that "geometry is of the devil" and "mathematicians should be banished as the authors of all heresies."

In spite of the condemnation of the Church during the late Middle Ages, a group of men, called alchemists, were toiling away, using whatever spare room they had available, in the eternal quest for the philosopher's stone: they were, of course, seeking the magic formula that could transform base metals into gold. These intrepid unsung pioneers, using primitive equipment and tinkering with potentially lethal chemicals, were the forerunners of the later scientists who, by trial and error, were able to discover chemical elements, a huge number of substances, and develop scientific and manufacturing processes that play a vital part in our lives today.

Apart from the eternal search for the precious shiny metal, the one thing which did capture people's imagination everywhere, in Europe, the Middle East and in China, was the observation and recording of astronomical data, the movement of the planets, the phases of the moon, the eclipses of the sun and the appearance of comets, all of which were unheralded heavenly occurrences, shrouded in mystery, which were often assumed to be portents of ill-luck. In fact, the development of more serious science began with astronomy and medicine. For more than one thousand years people in the Ancient Near East, Europe and Asia made use of the astrolabe, an ingenious device carefully designed to be used for predicting the positions of the sun, moon and stars as an aid in navigation, and, very importantly in those days, as a tool in astrological forecasting.

Although there did exist some translations of Arabic scientific texts – which were themselves translations of classical Greek ideas about science and medicine – there was little in the way of careful observation, hypothesis and experimentation, coupled with independent peer review and verification.

The ancient Greek geocentric conception of the cosmos (the idea that our planet Earth is at the very centre of the universe) was rigidly supported by the Church in the Middle Ages. In fact, the Dominican friar, mathematician and philosopher, Giordano Bruno, was accused of heresy and burned at the stake for suggesting that the sun did *not* go round the Earth. However, following the work of Copernicus in 1543, coupled with the invention of the telescope during the time of Galileo in the early 1600's, various people began to challenge the old ideas and, gradually, the Church began to loosen its vice-like grip on the scope and direction of scientific experimentation. This is in spite of the fact that some men in holy orders believed that the invention of the telescope "casts suspicion on the doctrine of the incarnation" and "the whole Christian plan of salvation" was being put at risk by people delving too deeply into the heavens.

The invention of the movable-type printing press by Johannes Gutenberg in 1440 had democratised learning – it allowed the faster propagation of new ideas and the gradual rejection of primitive Aristotelian science. The political upheavals in Europe during the 18th and early 19th centuries led to a new spirit, a movement which we now call the "Enlightenment", during which the old social order was replaced by ideals based upon human reason and a desire to test the veracity of beliefs which were previously considered sacrosanct. This was the spur which led to the numerous attempts at careful observation and the discovery of a variety of physical laws covering a whole range of issues, one of them leading to the gradual acceptance of the fact that we have a heliocentric solar system and the planets are constantly describing huge ellipses round our sun. We now know that our solar system consists of 9 planets, including Earth, although some cosmologists dismiss Pluto as a "dwarf planet".

Under the influence of Rene Descartes, Francis Bacon and Isaac Newton, there were heroic attempts at empirical mathematical science, coupled with deductive reasoning and the description of natural phenomena following careful observation. At the same time, scientists and philosophers, observing the fantastic diversity of animal, bird, reptile, insect and plant species, made various attempts at understanding the reasons for this rich and abundant diversity. (As an aside, the mind boggles at the profusion of beetle species existing today, estimated to total in excess of 350,000, each occupying a distinctive niche in the global ecosystem). In particular, people started looking for answers to a whole host of questions including: "How did mankind reach its present pre-eminent and dominant position in the world?"

Two hundred years ago Frenchmen such as Buffon, Laplace and Lamarck published their ideas about creation and evolution, while in England people were discussing the theories of Erasmus Darwin, who was a physician, biologist and natural philosopher. However the one person who has left an indelible mark in history was Charles Darwin, the grandson of Erasmus. His theory of evolution has already been described on page 35 (above).

In the previous chapter reference was made to the unusual phenomenon occurring during the period known as the Cambrian Explosion. For the sake of completeness it would be useful to set out the main geological time periods and the different new forms of life which are thought to have emerged in each of them.

PRE-CAMBRIAN PERIOD

The period of about 50 million years prior to the Cambrian is known as the Ediacaran, its name originating from the Ediacaran Hills of South Australia, where the fossils of microscopic blobs of small-bodied organisms were first found. They appear to have emerged after an intense glaciation period came to an end about 585 million years ago.

Originally, all primitive living organisms were split between two main "kingdoms": archaea and bacteria. These are both known as prokaryotes (single-celled creatures with no membrane-bound nucleus) and they were able to survive through the process of photosynthesis (using sunlight to create simple sugars). During the 3 billion years which preceded the Cambrian period there were 4 or 5 major periods which geologists have called "eons", when the only living creatures were tiny zooplankton (single-celled protozoa) and phytoplankton (bacteria and algae). And then, approximately 540 million years ago, the period known as the Cambrian Explosion commenced.

The initial creation and growth of all living things occurred in the oceans, rivers and lakes throughout the world. For a long time, any living thing could only function and survive if it existed within close proximity to water. In due course the detritus of the tiny living organisms and plants, which settled at the bottom of the oceans, combined with the hydrocarbon compounds which were part of the fabric of primordial Earth for billions of years, became converted into valuable substances, the "black gold" which we are now able to extract, refine and use as various grades of oil, gas and petroleum products.

As already mentioned, the different uses of these very important fossil fuels, which include the coal created during the subsequent Carboniferous period, have been very important for mankind's economic development and progress.

In pre-Cambrian times no living organisms were able to survive on dry land. Multi-celled creatures which were able to reproduce sexually only came into being about 1.2 billion years ago. Somewhat later, about 700 million years ago, sponges and fungi began to be created. My reading of the latest scientific theories indicates that sponges played an important role in creating the extraordinary richness in the fossil record which occurred during the subsequent Cambrian Explosion. Apparently, sponges harbour specialised bacteria which suck phosphorous out of seawater and, in turn, the sponges pump out significant quantities of oxygen-rich water. The continuing filtering and pumping action aerates the deep oceans and this assists in the growth of a variety of organisms and helps to create different species. Another reason for the increase in oxygen levels in pre-Cambrian times was the volume of phytoplankton. The action of burrowing into the sea-bed by the tiny micro-organisms causes a swirling of mud leading to the beneficial release of oxygen and minerals.

CAMBRIAN (540 TO 500 MILLION YEARS AGO)

The fossil record of the Cambrian period shows a distinct quickening in the pace of evolution and several new species are thought to have appeared for the first time during this geologically short period. Some creatures from the Cambrian period are called *trilobites*, a species of scavenging marine arthropods (invertebrate creatures) which roamed the oceans for 250 million years until they died out during the subsequent Permian period. Surprisingly, there are still some species of sea-creatures surviving today whose ancestors made their initial appearance hundreds of millions of years ago, one of them being the *lancelet*. Descendants of this tiny creature can still be found in the South China Sea. It has no brain, no skeleton, but it does have a backbone. Other examples of creatures which have managed to hang on since Cambrian times are the horse-shoe crab and certain species of starfish. It appears as though, at this stage, nature was prepared to sacrifice some mobility for the sake of the safety of an armour-plated exterior.

ORDOVICIAN (500 TO 440 MILLION YEARS AGO)

Scorpions and early arachnid species as well as shelled molluscs, oysters and clams appeared for the first time in this period. *Sea cucumbers*, a strange scavenging creature which still features in Chinese cuisine today, also began to appear. At the end of the Ordovician period planet Earth underwent a very severe ice age which lasted 500,000 years.

SILURIAN (440 TO 420 MILLION YEARS AGO)

It is thought that some bony fishes, the first creatures with a defined skeleton, made their appearance during this period. The very first land plants also began to get established.

DEVONIAN (420 TO 350 MILLION YEARS AGO)

This period saw the further development of major fish line-ages. Arthropods (invertebrate creatures, including insects, possessing segmented bodies) were the first animals to achieve the ability to live on dry land, away from water. This happened about 400 million years ago. According to the scientists, some fish began to mutate into primitive tetrapods, the earliest examples of four-limbed creatures. Unusual survivors from this period include the family of *lungfish*, some dating back 380 million years. Lungfish have the ability to breathe air and they have a well-developed skeleton. Other common species which began developing during this period include sharks and rays and this period also saw the development of ancestral amphibians, the early frogs, toads and salamanders. During the Devonian period major parts of the world became covered by dense vegetation and forests, with some trees growing up to 35 metres (over 120 ft.) tall.

CARBONIFEROUS (350 TO 290 MILLION YEARS AGO)

The beautiful spirally-shaped ammonites and free-swimming molluscs first appeared during this period. Another creature whose descendants still survive today is the *lamprey*, an eel-like parasitic fish with a jawless mouth. It lives in coastal and fresh waters and it obtains its nutrition by boring its mouth parts into the side of a host fish in order to suck its blood. King Henry I of England, the fourth son of William the Conqueror, is reputed to have "died from a surfeit of lampreys."

The Carboniferous period was also the age of the reptiles as well as major plant species. The development of the amniotic egg was an important evolutionary innovation because it allowed reptiles to move away from waterside habitats and they were able to colonize dry regions. During the latter part of this period there was a major ice age resulting in the degradation and decomposition of major plant species. The dense forests and woodlands which proliferated during the previous period died in great numbers and, eventually, they were compressed into huge deposits of coal in many parts of the world.

PERMIAN (290 TO 250 MILLION YEARS AGO)

During this period the major land masses in the southern hemisphere coalesced to form one supercontinent called *Pangaea*.

CHAPTER 3 EVOLUTION: THE LAST 540 MILLION YEARS

This, in turn, broke up after 100 million years to form the genesis of the continents with which we are familiar today. Some beetles and flies made their appearance for the first time about 270 million years ago. So, too, did the *gingko biloba* trees, which sport distinctive fan-shaped leaves and whose products are still being used in oriental medicine and food supplements. A major geological catastrophe occurred 250 million years ago, a period which is now termed "The Great Dying", when, according to some estimates, between 70% and 90% of all living creatures, both in the sea and on land, were wiped out. This was the result of the outpouring of huge quantities of lava and poisonous fumes from the Earth's core, a disaster which lasted thousands of years. There was massive climate change and the oceans reached high levels of toxicity.

TRIASSIC (250 TO 200 MILLION YEARS AGO)

The effects of the major geologic and climatic catastrophes which occurred during the previous period took thousands of years to be resolved. With the arrival of warmer and dryer conditions, crocodiles and turtles were able to thrive. Some dinosaurs began to appear 225 million years ago.

JURASSIC (200 TO 150 MILLION YEARS AGO)

This is the period which was dominated by the large number of dinosaurs, some of which were carnivorous. Some sharks, small mammals, amphibians as well as many flowering plants made their appearance for the first time. Until the evolution of bees in the subsequent Cretaceous period it was left to the beetles and other small insects (which first made their appearance during the Permian period) to carry out the vital work of pollination and propagation of plant species.

CRETACEOUS (150 TO 65 MILLION YEARS AGO)

There are more than 20,000 species of bees in the world, some of which appeared during this period. The end of this period is particularly noteworthy for the fact that a giant meteor, 10 kilometres in diameter, collided with planet Earth in the Yucatan region of Mexico. The huge climatic upheavals resulting from this impact led to the death of major species of small mammals and the smaller dinosaurs. This in turn led to the severe shrinkage of the food chain which had previously sustained the larger carnivorous dinosaurs which preyed on them. The only dinosaurs which were able to survive were the avian species which evolved into our modern birds.

TERTIARY (65 TO 2 MILLION YEARS AGO)

With the demise of the dinosaurs mammals took over as the largest life forms. Most of the animals, birds, insects and flowering plants which we recognise today had their origins in this period. The ancestors of modern elephants and ungulates (hoofed mammals such as horses, antelopes, cattle, sheep and other ruminants) began to emerge about 30 to 40 million years ago, soon after the availability of various grasses.

Less than 7 million years ago there was a "branching out" of some "rogue" mammalian genes away from the main ape stem, resulting in the evolving of a new species which we call hominids (almost human creatures), a cousin to the great apes. They evolved to become humankind's ancestors, as described in the next chapter.

QUATERNARY (2 MILLION YEARS AGO TO THE PRESENT)

Homo sapiens gradually became established as the dominant mammal barely 200,000 years ago, mainly due to their larger brain, their control of fire, the achievement of bipedalism and the acquisition of a special skill: verbal communication. There were repeated glaciation events in the preceding period, the latest one ending about 12,000 years ago. Mammoths, sabre-toothed tigers and other mega-fauna died out following the warming of the climate.

Evolution of Vertebrates

Reference has been made in the previous chapter to the unprecedented variety of animal and, particularly, marine creatures that first made their appearance during the period of the Cambrian Explosion, more than 500 million years ago. Since then, an evolutionary trajectory took hold which, on the principle of "survival of the fittest", resulted in the development of vertebrate animals which were better able to cope with the changed environment as well as the succession of extreme ice-ages and periodic droughts in different parts of the world. Placental mammals, which had been comparatively restricted in size and diversity until 65 million years ago, took advantage of the biological vacuum resulting from the disappearance of the dinosaurs, and they began to grow in size and complexity. Mammals were known to have existed more than 200 million years ago but they were small in size and variety.

The earliest mammalian fossil so far discovered by palae-ontologists (the scientists most closely involved in searching for and making sense of the fossil records) is the tiny skull of a *hadrocodium*, dating back to 195 million years ago, which was found in the Yunnan province of China. It was a mouse-like mammal, barely 2 inches in length. Unlike reptiles, which are cold-blooded, the hadrocodium and other primitive mammals were able to generate their own body heat. Many mammals developed a furry skin as a protection from the cold, and some acquired such valuable attributes as highly developed and specialised senses – ears, whiskers, larger eyes and echo-locating organs. As their foetuses were born alive, the mothers needed to acquire the ability to lactate in order to provide their offspring with the right nourishment.

The effect of planet Earth's collision with the massive asteroid 65 million years ago was apocalyptic. The asteroid was travelling at a speed more than 100 times faster than a jetliner and it struck our planet with such force that the carbon that is located deep in the Earth's crust liquefied. The atmosphere became blanketed by airborne carbon beads, while noxious clouds of dust caused widespread global fires. The sun's rays were obliterated for several years. Vast swathes of the Earth were poisoned by carbon monoxide, playing havoc with vegetation and the dinosaurs' food chain. The giant reptiles, the various dinosaurs, which had ruled unchallenged for 160 million years before that, died out completely, except for those which were able to fly and which eventually became the progenitors of the whole family of birds we see today.

Primates

The term "primates" is commonly used to refer to a group of more than 300 highly developed and distinctive species of placental mammals which first made their appearance on Earth about 60 million years ago, about 5 million years after the extinction of the dinosaurs. There is a huge variation in the size of primates – they range from the tiny mouse lemurs, weighing just a few grams, to the massive male lowland gorillas, which tip the scales at 150 kilos (well over 300 lbs). Some primates are mainly arboreal (monkeys, lemurs, shrews, bush babies, tarsiers, etc.) preferring to spend most of their lives moving about in the forest canopy, high above the ground, where they find adequate food and shelter from predators. Others, like the apes, gorillas, baboons and macaques, are primarily terrestrial. Primates inhabit every continent of the globe and they are found mainly in tropical and sub-tropical rain forests.

There is some fossil evidence which indicates that, about 25 million years ago, there occurred a spurt in the numbers and the evolutionary diversity in the population of "Great Apes", the group of mammalian primates which have no prehensile tails and to which humankind belongs. Palaeontologists have ascertained that during the Miocene epoch (which extended from about 23 million years ago to about 5 million years ago), there existed some twenty species of great apes. Nearly three quarters have since become extinct for a variety of reasons, such as loss of habitat, inability to cope with a changing environment, climate change or the result of interbreeding.

Today, the category of great apes is restricted to just five species: HUMANS, BONOBOS, CHIMPANZEES, GORILLAS and ORANGUTANS. These species are grouped together because their genome sequences are pretty similar and they are considered to be at the very top of mammalian evolution so far. In fact, we humans share about 98.5% of our gene pool with the bonobos.

CHAPTER 4

Emergence of Humankind

"It would be very difficult to explain why the Universe should have begun in just this way except as the act of God who intended to create beings (men and women) just like us."

Professor Stephen Hawking, *"A Brief History of Time"*

Scientists announced recently that if you were to compile a list of all the different species of insects, reptiles, birds, creatures of the sea and mammals, you would arrive at the grand total of some 8.7 million distinct non-bacterial species living today – although they were careful to point out that only a fraction of that number have been properly investigated and recorded. There may still be countless more living creatures of all categories, both in unexplored tropical forests and in the depths of the ocean, which await discovery. However, mammals (i.e. animals which give birth to live young) account for a very tiny fraction of this total – scientists have identified only about 6,000 genetically distinct species of mammals. They range from a tiny bat, no bigger than 1½ inches long, all the way up to the majestic 100 ft. (30 metres) blue whale, weighing 150 tons or more: the largest mammal that has ever lived.

Hominids

Recent research has demonstrated that *Homo sapiens*, anatomically modern mankind, have existed on planet Earth for barely 200,000 years – which, if the period since the creation of the universe were to be expressed in terms of a time-lapse of 24 hours, amounts to just a couple of seconds. Apparently, mankind last shared common ancestors with chimpanzees nearly 7 million years ago. Since then there have been some important physical developments which have resulted in the evolution of various hominids (almost human creatures).

As explained by the scientists who have followed Darwin, there was a "branching out" process between 6.5 million and 7 million years ago when, as a result of a sudden, unexplained chance gene mutation, there arose a new species, now called hominids, which later became the precursors of modern humans according to scientists. That was the point at which the human story can be said to have begun. A succession of hominids made their appearance, all of them having mutated from the central primate stem, and all being descendants of the long line of placental mammals which have evolved and diversified over the previous 60 million years. Scientists have been able to identify the following distinct species, all of which had their origins in North Africa and the Middle East:

HOMINID SPECIES	PERIOD (Millions of years ago)	SPECIAL FEATURES
Sahelanthropus Tchadensis	6.5	"Toumai" (fossil of earliest known hominid)
Ardipithecus Kadabba	6.0	Brain cavity 350 c.c.
Ardipithecus Ramidus	4.4	Discovered in Ethiopia
Australopithecus Anamensis	4.0	Attempt at bipedalism
Australopithecus Afarensis	3.5	"Lucy"; Brain cavity 600 c.c.
Homo Habilis	2.3	Use of simple tools
Homo Sediba	2.0	Improved diet
Homo Erectus	1.8	Brain cavity 900 c.c.
Homo Heidelbergensis	0.6	Ability to control fire. Most likely ancestor of modern mankind
Homo Neanderthalensis	0.3	Died out 30,000 years ago
Homo sapiens	0.2	Modern mankind. Brain cavity 1,350 c.c.

There have been almost 300,000 generations of hominids over the past 6.5 million years. During that time the brain cavity of hominids has grown from 320 to 1,350 cubic centimetres today.

It must be stressed that the above list does not purport to depict the complete linear evolution through time, from the most primitive hominid creatures to the present day *H. sapiens*. It would be wrong to believe that the above list is exhaustive and, very importantly, there is no indication that there was a single central unbroken line linking all the above species. Put another way, as regards the evolution of hominids, the term "family tree" may be better described as a "family bush", within which it is hard to discern how the several different species leading up to *H. sapiens* were interconnected in a biological way.

The dates shown above give only an approximate indication when the particular species acquired their distinctive physical characteristics. Each species became established as a result of an unplanned gene mutation and each had certain evolutionary advantages, but they died out for a variety of reasons, which are still not fully understood. Although modern mankind (*H. sapiens*) is the only hominid species existing today, it was not always so – in the past there were several species of hominids living in different geographical areas at the same time.

It is fair to state that Darwin never claimed that mankind is directly descended from apes, as alleged by some of his Victorian detractors. The truth is that mankind can be said to be cousins of the other great apes and we have been travelling along different, but closely related, gene trajectories.

Apparently, the cradle of human evolution was North East Africa – the first *H. sapiens* emerged as a distinct species in Chad, Ethiopia and the Rift Valley some 200,000 years ago. However, the cumbersome term *H. sapiens sapiens* is sometimes used in order to describe our present, more highly developed, cognitively symbolic and "meaning-seeking" nature. Apparently, our ancestors living 50,000 or 60,000 years ago were virtually indistinguishable from us both in physical stature and in mental capacity.

The Evolution of Hominids

What are the factors which may have led to the evolution of hominid species? There is evidence that there was a major change in the world's climate some 7 million years ago, leading to the development of savannah (temperate grasslands and woodlands) instead of the dense forests that existed before. This led some ape populations to leave the safety of the tree canopies and spend more time on the ground.

In time, one or two ape groups began to stand on their hind legs in order to have a better view of distant prey animals or to escape from potential predators. Another reason could be the need to regulate bodily temperature. Away from the shade of the trees, mammals need to keep cool. In the open grassland, if a quadruped is able to stand on its hind legs, its body is kept cooler because a smaller area is exposed to the scorching equatorial sun. Furthermore, in hot climates mammals depend on the evaporation of sweat to lose excess heat. As body fur impedes evaporation, this could be the main reason why hominids started to become smooth-skinned. There is another suggestion that, as hominids became more smooth-skinned, their offspring lost the ability to attach themselves to their parent's body fur and anchor themselves for safety. Hence the need for the parent to attempt bipedalism and carry their offspring in their arms while moving through the savannah or the forest floor.

The fossilised remains of the earliest known hominid, nicknamed *Toumai*, came to light in the African state of Chad within the last 25 years. Although scientists have found only badly crushed cranial material, they were able to conclude that Toumai had some humanlike features, such as smaller canine teeth. Some scientists (though not all), having examined the crushed cranium of Toumai, believe that although he was an arboreal creature for most of the time, he was probably a biped for some of the time, and they are prepared to accept that he represents the oldest ever hominid found to date.

It is believed that there was a more serious attempt at bipedal locomotion about 3.5 million years ago. In 1974 fossil hunters in Ethiopia discovered 40% of the skeleton of an unusual creature, which was later named *Lucy*. She stood just 1 metre tall (just over 3 ft.), she would have weighed less than 35 kilos (80 lbs.) and she is famous because the popular press refers to her as the "missing link" between apes and humans. She was neither an advanced form of ape nor a primitive form of human. Now labelled *Australopithecus Afarensis*, she belonged to a species which had certain ape and humanoid characteristics – the skull proportions were broadly ape-like, with a small brain case and a large projecting face. However, the canine teeth were reduced in size by comparison with other apes. Lucy belonged to a long-lived species of hominid which succeeded in surviving on earth for about 900,000 years before dying out.

H. Habilis (handyman) was able to fashion some simple tools and these were used to butcher prey. The purposeful crafting of stone implements, rather than just picking up and smashing any rocks they found lying around, which may have occurred some 2.5 million years ago, indicates that, even then, our hominid ancestors possessed a level of intelligence well in advance of even today's apes.

Apparently, the hominids that lived 2 million years ago gradually changed their diets – they switched from grasses and leaves to high-protein roots and tubers, as well as a small quantity of uncooked meat. *H. Erectus* had a brain cavity of about 900 cubic centimetres, lived in caves, and was the first hominid to leave Africa more than a million years ago, looking for new pastures.

H. Heidelbergensis, with a brain cavity of 1,200 c.c., appeared 600,000 years ago and it is believed that modern men and women (*H. sapiens*) have emerged as their eventual direct descendants. It appears that our distant ancestors first began to control fire and use it to cook their meat since that time, thus enabling them to consume a better and more varied diet which was higher in fat and protein – raw meat is much harder to digest. Inevitably, the introduction of more nutritious food contributed to their brain enlargement.

The first fossils of Neanderthal man were discovered in 1856 in the Neander valley of Germany. *H. Neanderthalensis*, a stocky and sturdy hominid with a receding forehead, a very prominent ridge above the eyebrows and a brain cavity of 1,400 c.c., flourished in Europe from about 300,000 years ago until the species died out about 30,000 years ago. During the last 20,000 years of their existence they must have lived and hunted in areas near those occupied by our own direct ancestors, *H. sapiens* (who had a brain cavity of 1,350 c.c.).

Neanderthals hunted cooperatively, using stone tools to butcher their prey, they kept their caves clean by separating their sleeping from their eating areas, they decorated their caves, used feathers as personal adornment and they buried their dead. However, in spite of their slightly larger brain, Neanderthals lacked various skills at coping with the changing climate and environment. They had only primitive language ability, their brains were not sufficiently developed to believe in an afterlife and, unlike *H. sapiens*, they left no clear artistic legacy. By contrast, *H. sapiens* had more imagination, better coping procedures and better hunting skills. Inevitably there was some inter-breeding. Some scientists believe that a significant proportion of European humans carry within their make-up about 4% of genes inherited from their Neanderthal cousins.

The world's ocean levels, climatic conditions and vegetation were quite different in those days and these geographical features facilitated the movement of creatures from one part of the globe to another in ways that would be more difficult today. In fact, there is evidence that primitive hominids such as *H. Erectus* began to leave Africa nearly 1.5 million years ago. They eventually reached Georgia (Caucasus), China, Java and even Australia. Anatomically modern humans arrived in Australia's

Northern Territory about 60,000 years ago and in Melanesia about 40,000 years ago.

There are some traces of hominid habitation in North America dating back more than 20,000 years.

Within the past few years the fossil of a small hominid creature was found on the island of Flores in Indonesia. It appears that this dwarf hominid, dubbed *H. Floriensis* (or the "Hobbit"), managed to exist on the island for about 80,000 years until as recently as 12,000 years ago, in the company of dwarf elephants and other creatures. There is some dispute as to whether it was a separate hominid species or whether it acquired its stunted growth as the result of the lack of certain nutrients in its diet.

It is certain that, for a long period of time, *H. sapiens* co-existed on earth with at least three other hominid species – *H. Erectus* in Asia, *H. Neanderthalensis* in Europe and the Middle East and *H. Floriensis* on the island of Flores in Indonesia.

Apes and Hominids Compared

If a palaeontologist is presented with a collection of fossils, and he/she is asked to decide whether they belonged to an ape or one of the more advanced hominid species, there are certain obvious clues. And here I am indebted to Ian Tattersall, whose very informative book, *"Masters of the Planet"*, provided the facts supporting these notes.

Hominids had larger faces which were less protruding than those of the apes. They had receding foreheads and forward-directed eyes, and they had mobile arms which they could freely rotate at the shoulder joint. Hominids had smaller canine teeth as compared with apes and their molar teeth had thick enamel with robust jaws, thus allowing them to eat a broader range of forest foods. Ape and hominid hands may look super-ficially similar, but apes have longer hands, suitable for grasping branches, and much shorter thumbs in relation to the fingers. Hominids had opposable thumbs – we modern *H. sapiens* have the most dexterous hands, possessing the unique and valuable facility of placing our thumbs across our palms, making it easy to pick up and manipulate tiny objects, an attribute denied to apes.

In order to climb trees and navigate their way through the canopy an ape's ankle bones need to be very flexible because its feet need to grasp branches and twigs. Hominids (and, most certainly, mankind) have lost that flexibility.

All vertebrates have an aperture in their cranium to enable the spinal cord to be connected to the brain. In quadrupeds such as apes this cavity, known as the *foramen magnum*, is located at the rear of the skull and it faces backwards. This means that a quadruped's skull hangs on the front of a horizontal spine. By contrast, the aperture of a more-advanced biped like us is located on the underside of the skull and it faces downwards, so that the skull balances atop an erect vertical spine.

An important clue as to whether fossils belong to an ape or a hominid is provided by examining the pelvic area. The more advanced hominid's pelvis is wider and flatter than the ape's, making it better able to support bipedal locomotion. In anatom-ically modern humans the iliac blade is shorter and wider – this is a requirement for maintaining the centre of gravity while walking. The gradual widening of the humanoid pelvis is designed to facilitate the passage of the newborn – this feature became increasingly important due to the fact that there has been a gradual increase in cranial size over the last 2 million years. It is worth noting that the females of the more modern hominids had a birth canal which was smaller than that of the knuckle-walking apes.

As already indicated, the brains of all hominids were characteristically larger than those of other great apes. In fact, most scientists were originally inclined to assert that an animal with a brain volume of at least 750 cubic centimetres could belong to the genus *Homo*, but this rigid criterion has now been abandoned. The gradual improvement in hominid diets led to their acquisition of a brain which was larger and better developed than that of other creatures. Although the brain takes up only 2% of our body's mass, it consumes about 20% of the body's energy, so it requires higher grade nutrition to sustain and develop it.

As the most evolutionarily advanced hominid, we modern men and women possess the capacity to use our brains more efficiently to handle information, we retain a vast store of facts and opinions as memory, we seek meaning to our lives and we ask the question: why? Other creatures rely mainly on their inherited instincts, as well as on what they can see, smell, hear, taste and feel at that particular moment. By contrast, mankind's mental faculties enable us to imagine and "think outside the box". The acquisition of our unique sensibility, resulting from our larger brain, seems to have occurred rather abruptly and very recently (apparently, only about 60,000 years ago).

The Power of Speech

The other vital attribute of humankind is our superior voice-box, which was also acquired fairly recently. We have the unique capacity to express ourselves in speech and we are able to convey our thoughts in an unambiguous way. Language defines us clearly, and it has been absolutely crucial in our progression from bipedal hominid to modern man and woman. It has given us the capacity to control our environment and maintain our dominance over other creatures.

The evolution of language is a topic which divides scientists. Naturally, the relevant developments and evolution of our capacity for language have left no historical traces; nobody has put forward coherent explanations as to why and how the attribute of speech came about. It has recently been discovered that Neanderthals had acquired the capacity for primitive speech during their early development. The original belief was that Neanderthals could only rely on grunts as well as visual signals and gestures, but this notion has had to be slightly revised as a result of recent research.

Why is it that today only humans possess the power of speech? Other animals rely on non-verbal communication, such as the special waggle-dance of bees in a hive to pinpoint the location of nectar, the shrieks and howls of most monkeys, the chest-thumping of lowland gorillas, the slap of a dolphin's tail on the water surface, the subtle scent-marking or visual signals and gestures of many mammals. Many insects secrete pheromones to send signals to members of their own species. However, they all lack the necessary prerequisites, the shape of their vocal tract and larynx, for the enunciation of words. The muscles in the face, tongue, and mouth are all controlled by the brain. In addition, it is believed that *H. sapiens* acquired a specialised language gene, FOXP2, which underwent a mutation about 100,000 years ago. Vocalisation improved when we began to use our tongue to modulate sound. The need to communicate verbally became ever more important when humans began to live in family groups, thus facilitating communal activities, such as tool-making, shelter construction, animal husbandry and agriculture.

Our ability to construct complex symbolic and abstract speech, which enables us to understand each other with a high degree of precision, in unique among mammals.

Triumph of Modern Mankind

What is the secret of the success of our own species, *H. sapiens*? As indicated above, mankind has been able to become masters of our environment due to 4 important factors: firstly, our ability to achieve bipedalism, secondly, our mastery over fire, enabling our ancestors to eat more digestible, nutritious and varied diets, thirdly, our larger brain, and, fourthly, our unique and advanced capacity to communicate using speech.

The hominids' ability to walk upright, the sustained use of fire for warmth as well as for culinary purposes, the shaping and usage of stone tools, the devising of ever more advanced techniques for trapping and killing prey, the ability to seek out edible plants and roots and their skill in building hearths, camp fires and shelters, all these were valuable attributes which developed randomly and which, over the millennia, have been inherited by today's men and women.

If, six million years ago, you had posed the question, "Which animal species are the most likely to survive and dominate the planet in the future?" you would not have naturally assumed that modern mankind would feature in any list of candidates. Compared to other species that existed 200,000 years ago, you could not have guessed that *H. sapiens* would survive for long, let alone become the masters over the environment and be the most successful of all hominids. We are not endowed with outwardly visible natural advantages as compared with other mammals. Mankind is devoid of sharp teeth or claws to hunt for food or put up a convincing fight against bigger and more fearsome creatures. Most of our potential predators can easily outrun us. Our babies are born pitifully defenceless and they are in need of close and sophisticated parental nurturing for the first dozen years. Yet we have survived and we have succeeded in exploiting the natural resources of planet Earth to our advantage.

Our brains have virtually doubled in size over the past 2 million years, (although, it must be said, tree shrews have a higher brain-to-body ratio than any other mammals, including humans). Our brain's size and complexity has made us inventive, adventurous and resilient. We learnt to tame wolves and we mutated them into dogs, which we use as pets, as companions and as helpers in certain defined situations. We have adapted wild cattle, sheep, buffaloes, horses, camels, even llamas for use in our farms, for food, for transport as well as beasts of burden. We learnt to breed poultry to provide cheap protein. We have been able to devise a bewildering range of medicines, originating from nature, and we have been able to prolong our life expectancy. More than anything else, mankind has acquired the important capacity of processing information, thinking in symbols and recognising patterns. We are also good at exercising our imagination and making plans for the future.

Very importantly, the human diet underwent a radical improvement some 12,000 years ago. Until then our ancestors ate the meat of land mammals, eggs, nuts and fruit. Gradually several cereals were introduced. These included an early ancestor of wheat called emmer, which thrived in areas now known as Iran and Iraq. Rice became the staple Chinese diet, while maize grew abundantly in Central America. Potatoes have been cultivated in Peru for at least 7,000 years. These foods began to replace the primitive tubers which were the main carbohydrate sources in the past.

If you ask the question: "Has mankind reached the peak of physical perfection and has the process of evolution come to an end?" the answer must be that evolution will continue as before but, as far as *H. sapiens* are concerned, the process of evolution by natural selection will be replaced by a process of evolution by human intervention. One interesting phenomenon has been highlighted recently by Professor Bruce Hood of Bristol. He is reported as saying that the human brain has been shrinking for the past 20,000 years, "probably as a result of domestication". The average male brain, which measured 1,500 c.c. then, now measures an average of 1,350 c.c. Professor Hood suggests that this shrinkage is the result of a shift from a hunter-gatherer life-style towards living in a close-knit agriculture community.

In France, Spain and elsewhere our ancestors have bequeathed to us artistic images on the ceilings and walls of caves which are outstanding in their sophistication. The images are found in several locations including Castillio (Spain), Chauvet (France) and Altamira (Spain). The series of paintings which captured many people's imagination are found in Lascaux (France), where the outstanding decorations are thought to date from 20,000 to 30,000 years ago, a time of cool summers and long harsh winters.

These beautiful images, mostly depicting animals, such as aurochs, deer and bison, but also including abstract designs, first came to light about 150 years ago and they are the handiwork of hunter-gatherers who felt impelled to record the images for posterity. The images, which have miraculously survived several millennia, are testimony to the wonderful and unique human creative spirit, powered by our sophisticated brain.

In October 2014 the press and TV media reported that some astonishingly sophisticated cave paintings had come to light in Sulawesi, formerly known as the Celebes, one of the Indonesian islands. The most recent discoveries are thought to date from 40,000 years ago and consist of beautiful limestone stencils and paintings of a hand as well as some carefully drawn depictions of prehistoric animals. They are considered among the oldest figurative art works in the world.

Some anthropologists have suggested that all these cave paintings and images, whether in Europe, South Africa or South East Asia, demonstrate a belief in unseen spirits and could be the result of an attempt by our ancestors to make sense of the

world around them. The pictures were not merely representa-
tional – there is real artistic skill and symbolism in some of the
designs. They were very meaningful and some were probably
meant to create a link with people on the move. They could be
seen as indicative of a religious or spiritual feeling, an attempt
to make contact with an unseen power or a deity.

CHAPTER 5

The Road to Monotheism

"What I see in Nature is a magnificent structure that we can comprehend only very imperfectly, and that must fill a thinking person with a feeling of humility. This is a genuinely religious feeling that has nothing to do with mysticism."

Albert Einstein, physics Nobel Laureate

Scientists tell us that 50,000 years ago our ancestors were little different from modern humans, both physically and mentally. Of course, they had vastly different problems to contend with. For *Homo sapiens*, living in the harsh realities of the time, either on the savannah or, much later, as members of agricultural or fishing settlements, their most pressing concerns revolved round the constant hunt for food and the avoidance of danger. Inevitably, in such primitive circumstances, the laws of the jungle prevailed, with nature red in tooth and claw. The moral standards and the dining habits of our ancestors could have been hardly more edifying than those of the aggressive and noisy hyenas or the squabbling vultures hungrily devouring the freshly-killed carcass of a gazelle, as depicted in a natural history documentary film.

Gradually, as the population grew, it was necessary to pay greater attention to the choreography of living in larger communities which began to change in character. Rights and obligations had to be more carefully defined and it was necessary to think about a greater division of labour and responsibilities. Questions of reciprocity came to the fore and concepts of moral behaviour had to develop in order to cope with the quickening pace of life. Before any of the major religions began to influence the behaviour of ordinary people there seems to have been a set of seven "Noachide Laws" which, in primitive societies, were deemed to be enough to enable people to live in tolerable amity. These consisted of a group of moral imperatives which, according to an ancient tradition, were given to "the children of Noah", i.e. to all humanity. These laws specifically prohibited idolatry, murder, theft, sexual immorality and blasphemy. Furthermore, the consumption of meat cut out from a living animal was totally disallowed and, finally, the laws called for the speedy establishment of proper courts of law in every society. In the absence of organised religion, these "laws" may have served a useful purpose. One wonders, though, whether these laws were observed more in the breach than in the observance.

This chapter is devoted to sketching out the belief systems of different peoples in many parts of the world, as revealed by my actual visits to some geographical locations and my own independent research. There then follows an account of the genesis of monotheism, the revolutionary faith and belief structure which supplanted the paganism, animism and the superstitious practices which have come down from pre-history. Naturally, one can only skim the surface of this vast and fascinating subject.

Ancient Beliefs and Religious Practices

In pre-history, side by side with the Noachide laws, there has always existed a set of beliefs and codes of conduct, some of which would perhaps be regarded today as weird, if not downright perverse, unethical or even criminal. In the absence of strong centralised government and a trustworthy legal system, for example, some ancient thinkers believed that "good" or "bad" behaviour was judged according to whether an action was "approved" or "disapproved" by the elders or by society at large. This is, of course, an imprecise and blurred objective, it was easily open to corruption or abuse, and it provided an opportunity for thuggish or unprincipled behaviour by those in authority.

Five or six thousand years ago the most sophisticated societies in the world were taking root in six main regions: Egypt, Mesopotamia, Greece/Rome, the Indus Valley, China and Mesoamerica. There were relatively large population centres in parts of the Middle East and India, where those in power maintained their hegemony over sizeable geographical areas. In China an advanced civilisation started developing 6,000 years ago, centred round the mighty Yangtze and Yellow Rivers. The geographical area which we call Mesoamerica included certain parts of modern-day Mexico, Bolivia, Guatemala, Nicaragua and other areas in central and south America; they consisted of more sparsely-populated communities which were, in the main, isolated from one another. Some of the terrain was inaccessible and mountainous, although river navigation enabled a modicum of contact between the peoples.

It would be fair to say that, up to about 4,000 years ago, the religious beliefs and practices throughout the known world can best be described as pagan or animist, where the celestial bodies were the object of their devotions, and where various animals (crocodiles, scarab beetles, cows, serpents and elephants) were accorded spiritual status, while geographical features such as mountains, caves and rivers became designated as sacred sites.

In ancient **Egypt** religion played a crucial part in the life of the people. The worship of the various gods and goddesses, including the sun god Ra and the creator god Amun, dominated every aspect of life. Elaborate rituals and expert mummification skills were used as a way of honouring the dead and these have been remarkably successful in preserving the cadavers to this day. Pyramids were constructed at Heliopolis (otherwise known as *Ein Shams* in Arabic), the centre of the sun-god rituals, where the Pharaohs were entombed. The Pharaohs were considered to have had the status of a god, although they mirrored humanity in their habits.

The belief was that death was merely a transitional stage in the progress towards a better life and that, at some time in the future, there would be a rebirth: to that end, valuable objects, including gold, were placed in the tomb.

A sophisticated polytheistic culture arose about 5,500 years ago around the Tigris and Euphrates rivers in southern **Mesopotamia**, now called Iraq. The Sumerian city states were under the control of theocratic governments and a variety of priests were charged with the diffusion of religious and cultural traditions. The main Sumerian deities were Anu (god of heaven), Entil (god of the air), Enki (god of male fertility) and Inanna (goddess of warfare).

The Sumerian and the nearby Akkadian peoples were living in a region which is now generally considered to have been the cradle of world civilization as we understand it. The Sumerian people invented the potter's wheel and they used yeast to make bread and beer. The chariot wheel was a development which the Sumerians pioneered and they used domesticated horses to pull their chariots into battle. The wheels were originally made of solid wood but they were later improved by the use of bronze. It is believed that the invention of cuneiform writing (wedge-shaped impressions on clay tablets) developed here about 5,000 years ago.

It is estimated that, altogether, the Sumerians and the Akkadians numbered 1.5 million, out a total world population of less than 30 million. The city of Uruk became the most urbanised city in the world with a population exceeding 50,000.

The life of the Sumerian people was dominated by a very ancient legend – the Epic of Gilgamesh. He was King of Uruk and was believed to have been part god and part man. Incorporated in the epic is a story which predates that of Noah and the Great Flood.

The legend relates that the gods decided to flood the earth because the people made so much noise that it disturbed their sleep.

Before the advent of Christianity, people living in the Greco-Roman Empire were idol worshippers (except, of course, for the Israelites living in the territories of Israel and Judah). They relied heavily on signs, omens and the pronouncements of soothsayers for guidance in their day-to-day lives. For the best part of 1,000 years until about 400 CE Greek and Roman society followed a pagan way of life, where sorcery, magic, divination and astrology were inextricably woven into their lives. There was an extensive mythology and a strong belief in Olympian gods and goddesses, one of them being Zeus, king of the gods who was responsible for sending thunder and lightning. Although the Greek gods were immortal they still had to obey fate. There was a strong belief in an underworld, the resting place of the spirits of the dead.

There was no unified religion and it was left to several wise men to devise their own rules and establish their own learned academies. Great philosophers such as Socrates, Plato and Aristotle developed a stream of high-blown precepts and offered instruction in such diverse topics as philosophy, democracy, mathematics, drama, oratory, poetry and architecture but there was no attempt at combining individual teachings to create a morality-based coherent religion. The Greek philosophers emphasised democracy and ethics, but what was lacking was the warmth of interpersonal relationships. Very importantly, society did not have a religious underpinning.

In Homer's age people subscribed to a culture which put a premium on bodily strength and courage. In 363 BCE Theognis expounded ideas which, from the vantage point of today's morality, we would regard as unprincipled and wrong. For example, he wrote:

"Beguile your enemies with fair words, but when you have him within your grasp, wreak your wrath on him, and let no scruples stand in your way."

Ancient Greeks did not recognise any connection between morality and religion. Their primitive mythical gods, representations of which were carved out of stone or wood, were not moral agents to be venerated as the unswerving champions of righteousness. Instead, they were vindictive and inscrutable, to be conciliated and appeased. Euripides considered the concept of hope as anathema, and it was one of the evils contained in Pandora's Box. The stoic philosophy posited that contentment and serenity were to be valued above other virtues. In pre-Socratic times the morality of the Greeks rested upon custom rather than upon principle, and, of course, we are all aware that hedonism preached the virtues of maximum pleasure and minimum pain. Epicureanism became equated with depravity and licentiousness. Greek and Roman temples resorted to vile and lewd methods of "worship", including the use of temple prostitutes.

Perhaps the one aspect of morality which we would find most abhorrent today is that Greco-Roman society, aided and abetted by such luminaries as Plato, not only justified the practice of infanticide, but they also approved the deliberate neglect of aged and infirm people who were considered to be of no further use. These cast-offs from general society were left to perish outdoors and on hillsides, at the mercy of the elements and wild animals.

In fact, Tacitus, a Roman senator and historian who lived in the first century of the Common Era, mockingly referred to the fact that the Jews were stupid enough to allow any baby born with a deformity to live and grow normally, rather than follow the accepted Roman practice of deliberately disposing of it at birth.

It was not until the early part of the fourth century of the Common Era that the pagan Roman Emperor Constantine formally converted to Christianity, which soon became the dominant religion of the day.

Three thousand miles away from Europe the people living in the River Ganges delta in **India** were developing their faith. The early form of Hinduism did not possess any ideas of social progress and there was little or no attempt made to develop human personality. Hindu society is stratified and it legitimises social systems based on privilege. The idea of any advancement in any temporal or social sense was alien. In early Hindu philosophy it was meritorious to forego all desire, all ambition, and to seek dissolution of selfhood and individuality, in the same way as a raindrop is dissolved in a bucketful of water.

A chief feature of Hinduism is the belief in the three gods who rule the world: Brahma (the creator), Vishnu (the preserver), and

Shiva (the destroyer). There are other gods, such as Ganesha, the elephant-headed patron deity of commercial enterprise and Lakshmi, the goddess of fortune.

There is also a strong Hindu belief in transmigration or rebirth. Reincarnation is central to the elaborate caste system, with bad people being punished for their sins by being relegated to a lower societal caste. Every act, good or bad, finds its reward, not only in heaven but also in hell.

The Shang Dynasty in **China**, established around 3,500 years ago, encouraged the development of innovations such as writing, bronze metallurgy and architecture. Chinese philosophy, closely allied to religion, laid great stress upon ancestor worship and, very crucially, the importance of establishing a harmonious relationship with nature. In particular, a god named Shangti was venerated as "The Great Ancestor". A tradition of great literature, art and philosophy began to develop from the time of Confucius (born 551 BCE).

Buddhism, which has been the central tenet of most Chinese people for nearly 2,000 years, is not founded on the belief in a deity. Buddhists venerate a human being, Siddhartha Gautama, who was born approximately 2,500 years ago. Buddhists attempt to lead their lives according to his teachings. Followers of Buddha (the enlightened one) are encouraged to cultivate introspection and a contemplative frame of mind.

In ordinary life people are encouraged to adopt the "eightfold path", devised by Buddha, so that one can reach a state of enlightenment, *Nirvana*, a release from suffering, a state of blissful egolessness, serenity and imperturbable stillness of mind. Enlightenment's supreme objective is the ability to meditate on the formless and the non-physical, in order to achieve quiescence and non-action. When you eliminate the pressures caused by ceaseless physical or material cravings you will be free of needless vexations. Belief in God is of minor importance to Buddhists; the main objective is to devise ways to escape from the suffering which is ever-present in our lives. The act of worship involves the offering of fragrant incense, gifts of rice as well as appropriate prayers.

According to Buddhist belief death is not the end of life – it is merely the end of the body we inhabit in this life. Our spirit lives on and will become attached to a new body and a new life. Therefore, we should not fear death because there will a rebirth later on.

In **Mesoamerica** the dominant pre-Christian cultures were Olmec, Tiwanaku, Teotihuacan, Maya, Inca and Aztec, and the emphasis was on the worship of several gods, mainly related to the sun and agriculture. In 1519 Hernan Cortes and his Spanish *conquistadores* invaded Mexico and soon dominated many areas of Central and South America. Before the Spanish conquest the people had followed their ancient pagan practices. For example, in the area now known as Bolivia, where the Tiwanaku were established for hundreds of years, the god of action was Viracocha, the shaper and destroyer of many worlds. The belief was that he created people out of rock and brought them to life through the earth. Viracocha was powerful enough to create giants capable of moving massive stones.

The one name which I remember with fascination and awe from my history studies in school was Montezuma, also known as Moctezuma, the mighty Aztec emperor. In time, I became intrigued by everything to do with Mexico and Brazil in particular. I studied their strange art forms and I was fascinated by the beautifully symmetrical, cone-shaped volcano called Popocatepetl as well as the dense tropical jungles, teeming with exotic wildlife, through which the mighty Amazon River flows. Many years later I achieved my ambition to visit Mexico and I travelled to see the wonderfully impressive pyramids and other archaeological treasures which date from more than 2,000 years ago.

During my visit I learnt that, many centuries before the advent of the Aztecs in Mexico, an important civilisation called Teotihuacan had existed, centred 40 kilometres (25 miles) away from the modern metropolis of Mexico City. The area rose to prominence around 100 BCE. By the year 500 CE the population was estimated to total 100,000 and it was certainly one of the two biggest cities in the contemporary world. This is an amazing statistic considering that London's population did not reach that figure until 1500 CE.

During my trip I was able to see several pyramid structures, such as the Pyramid of the Sun (one of the largest in the world), the Pyramid of the Moon and the Pyramid of the Feathered Serpent. All these pyramids were related to individual deities, the chief being a god called Tlaloc. Another important deity was the Great Goddess, while others included the Storm God, the War God and the god dedicated to the Netted Jaguar. One of their charming beliefs was that time only had only begun "when the crocodile emerged from the river."

In 536 CE the catastrophic eruption of Ilopango volcano in what is now the modern state of El Salvador resulted in the breakdown of established society. Crops failed and the peoples' trust in religion vanished overnight. The city of Teotihuacan was almost reduced to rubble by the subsequent rioting of its inhabitants, who went about putting various important structures to the torch. The number of people who lived in the area dwindled to 20,000.

By the year 600 CE the formerly vibrant ancient culture was no more, their religious practices having become moribund, while emigration to other localities gathered pace. It took another 600 years for the area to be resettled and developed again, this time by the Aztecs.

The Mesoamerican people had been told by their priests that child sacrifice was necessary in order to propitiate the gods of rain and agriculture. Children were collected from all over the country, carried in litters and brought to a place of sacrifice. There they were put to death and their blood was splattered on statues of the various deities.

The Incas soon became the largest native empire in the New World controlling the vast area from Colombia to Central Chile in South America with a population of some 10 million. They believed that lightning, earthquakes, volcanic eruptions and fertility were all controlled by a panoply of gods, the chief being Inti who made agriculture possible. In an Argentinean museum today there is the display of the mummy of a fifteen-year-old Inca girl who, 600 years ago, had been drugged with coca leaves, plied with alcohol and left to freeze to death high in the Andes. She had been a sacrificial offering designed as homage to the deities in order to ensure adequate rainfall.

As part of the climax of certain annual Aztec festivals, many hundreds of young men and women had their wrists and feet bound, their chests were then slashed open with sharp tools made of obsidian (smooth lava rock) and their beating hearts were then torn out and shown to the people, all this in honour of the sun god. The Aztecs believed that the sacrificial victims would join the sun god in paradise.

Visits to Modern Places of Worship

One of the things I like to do when I am travelling is to allow time to visit a different place of worship, irrespective of religion or denomination, in order to get an impression of how different people commune with the spiritual forces and the deities which form an inseparable part of their lives. What follows below is a very brief account of what I was able to observe.

The area I know best is South East Asia, New Zealand and the South Pacific, as my work at the time necessitated extensive travel there. In Singapore, within walking distance of the 140-year old Maghain Aboth synagogue, my wife and I visited the Sri Krishnan Hindu temple in Waterloo Street, which is situated right next door to the Kwan Im Thong Hood Cho Chinese temple. The elaborately carved sandstone representations of the Hindu deities, the glow of the temple lights, the sandalwood incense rising from the various agarbattis and the chanting of the devotional prayers inside the Hindu house of prayer, all served as a hauntingly spiritual backdrop to the sight of the Chinese Buddhist worshippers, waving joss-sticks in a ritual manner, before placing them in a beautifully decorated urn filled with sand. The intermingling of the prayers of the two religions, men and women of all ages performing their distinctive devotions within a mere 20 yards of each other, represented a heartwarming demonstration of harmony, an object lesson in racial and religious tolerance.

On another occasion, during the Hindu festival of Thaipusam, I went very early to Upper Serangoon Road and, subsequently, to the other temple in Tank Road, to watch Tamil devotees being smeared with grey ash and, after they had been inducted into a trance-like state, various parts of their torsos were pierced with sharp metal hooks attached to little brass bells. Large skewers were pushed through both cheeks of the devotees, and they began their long barefoot walk of penance. I spoke to one Tamil bystander who explained that he himself underwent the same procedure some ten years earlier. He had submitted to the ordeal, in fulfilment of a vow he had made, after his daughter, who was seriously ill, made a complete recovery following an accident.

My wife and I were invited to witness Muslim Malay weddings in Kuala Lumpur and we have watched the ancient practice of decorating Chinese Buddhist funeral shrines with paper and bamboo models of cars and other "valuable" objects and fruit, especially oranges.

I enjoyed taking part in a Friday night Sabbath service in the tiny jewel of a synagogue in Malaga in southern Spain, where they use the traditional Ladino-style mode of prayer. Over the years, at one time or another, I have observed the congregation at Sunday worship in Singapore's St. Andrew's Anglican Cathedral, and my wife and I sat among the worshippers celebrating the New Year in the impressive Roman Catholic cathedral in Seville, where we were all requested to greet and shake hands with the worshippers seated around us. On another occasion I was invited to address a Christian evangelical fellowship service. I described the essential beliefs and practices of the Jewish religion and I was soon caught up in their enthusiastic and highly demonstrative mode of worship. There were spontaneous cries of "Praise be the Lord!", "Amen to that!" and "Halleluiah!" during my address to the congregation.

During a few days' holiday on the beautiful island of Bali we visited a Pura (Balinese temple) set amidst the coconut palms and the beautifully sculpted and well-irrigated rice-growing terraces. We listened to the sound of a small group of musicians beating hypnotically on their Gamelan instruments, while a succession of young girls walked in silent procession, carrying rice and other foodstuffs. They looked impressive, wearing their richly decorated traditional costume, and they had frangipani and bougainvillea blooms woven delicately into their sleek black hair.

In Bali the dominant religion is a variation of Hindu belief in gods and demigods with an interesting amalgam of Muslim Malay and animist traditions. The people belong to one of nine sects and there is a caste system, as in Hinduism. They believe that every element of nature possesses its own powers as well as its own gods and goddesses. A tree, a bowl of rice, even a bolt of recently woven Batik cloth, they are all potential homes for spirits whose energy can be directed either for good or evil.

I have derived huge personal benefit and I have learnt a lot from my visits to all the different places of worship. On many such occasions, while observing the devotions of different people in their own temple, church or shrine, I did experience a new spiritual insight, a communion with my Maker and an echo of my own beliefs and prayers, even though I did not share their faith and I did not fully understand their language and imagery. I have come to appreciate and admire the intense religiosity of people all over the world who have devised their own paths to expressing their devotion to their deity.

The Advent of Monotheism

We have seen that, during the primal darkness of pre-history, people were led to believe that deities were represented by a variety of supernatural creatures. A virtuous way of life was achieved by the examination of animal entrails, consulting oracles and making visits to sacred sites. Many cultures needed to carry out some form of human sacrifice of able-bodied men, women and unwanted children, innocent blood being dedicated to different gods which needed to be propitiated.

Out of this miasma of myths, folktales and the pronounce-ments of soothsayers there arose one outstanding person who transformed the nature of religion by initiating the belief in the one unseen God. His name was Abraham the son of Terach, who was a carver of pagan idols, and who was born some 3,900 years ago in Ur of the Chaldees, Mesopotamia (now called Iraq).

According to the traditions of Judaism, Christianity and Islam, Abraham had a spiritual encounter with the Almighty after which he accepted the call to renounce his pagan family beliefs, to strike out on his own and to have faith in the one God. The Almighty made a covenant with Abraham and directed him to travel to the land of Canaan, the land which we now call Israel, there to be "the father of a great nation."

Initially, Abraham and his descendants were called Hebrews (derived from the word *HABIRU*, meaning the people from the other side of the river) but, after a few generations, they became known as Israelites. The latter name stemmed from the fact that Israel was the alternative name for Jacob, Abraham's grandson. Today the three Abrahamic faiths consider that they are spiritually descended from Abraham.

Because of the threat of famine in Canaan, the descendants of Abraham and their extended families migrated to the land of Egypt. The annual flooding of the Upper Nile provides many areas of Egypt's delta with richly productive deposits of silt suitable for growing a variety of crops. Initially, the children of Israel were tolerated and their numbers flourished. But, after the accession of a new Pharaoh, the Israelites were forced into a period of slavery which lasted 210 years. About 3,300 ago Moses, the Israelite leader, who was brought up in the Egyptian royal court, was directed by God to lead his people away from Egypt and travel to the Promised Land of Israel.

Freedom from slavery was only accomplished after God had caused ten plagues to befall Egypt. During their long march of freedom Moses communed with God on Mount Sinai and he received the Torah (also known as the Five Books of Moses) which now forms the core of Jewish belief and practice. That was the start of religion based on monotheistic belief. Much later, the followers of Christianity and Islam warmed their hearts and nourished their soul by the glow of the brazier lit by

THE STORY OF HUMANKIND

the Hebrew Bible. Both these daughter religions are monotheistic and they have both borrowed several features from Judaism.

Many of the original biblical personalities are revered equally by all three religions.

In time, the monotheistic religions steered the people away from the barbarism that existed all around them. Three thousand years ago the Israelites were successful in attracting numerous converts who eschewed the pagan beliefs and the body-worshipping cult of the ancient Greeks and, later, the gaudy ostentation and ruthlessness of ancient Rome. Today, the beliefs and way of life of close to one-half of the world's population have been influenced, one way or the other, by the teachings which have their roots in the Abrahamic tradition.

The Torah

The Torah is a record of the early life and development of the Hebrews/Israelites who, over the course of many centuries, forged a direct relationship with God. The Torah is also a treasury of religious maxims and precepts, all set out with the clear objective of diffusing ethical ideas and good standards of behaviour. It is worth emphasising that the Torah was not given to a select band of heavenly angels, who would have been leading a blameless life anyway, but to mortal and fallible mankind, who have to learn to negotiate their way through seemingly insurmountable odds, and face the remediable evils of life as best they can on a daily basis. Some Torah passages are presented in a poetic or allegorical or mythical form, in keeping with the tradition of the time. The bare text does not give up its full meaning on first reading, so it was left to our prophets and sages to tease out the full impact of the words. Tom Goldingray, in his book, "*Approaches to Old Testament Interpretation*," says that the Torah and the relevant interpretations "must be seen as something that both describes and prescribes faith." And Robin Routledge, in his volume, *"Old Testament Theology,"* writing about the centrality of the Torah to the Jewish people, says:

> *"It is more than a description of what God's people believed in the past: it is also normative for the faith of God's people in the present. It sets out what we should believe. It contains creedal statements, affirmations and principles vital to our faith today."*

The Torah says that mankind was "created in the image of God," implying that humans are, in some way, different in dignity and status from other living animals. We are imbued with spiritual qualities, which include free will, the power of imagination and the possession of authority over the rest of creation. The following is the relevant biblical quotation:

> *"Let us make man in our image, after our likeness, and let them have dominion ... over all the earth."*

> *Genesis, chapter I, verse 26*

The Special Attributes of Mankind

CHAYAH is a Hebrew word meaning a living thing, whether a human or animal. There then occurs a trio of words which are sometimes inter-changeable but whose meaning can be carefully distinguished. All human and animal life can be said to have a NEFESH, which is sometimes described as instinct, and which relates to our physical actions and attributes; it includes the need of all creatures for nutrition and growth.

In addition, unique among all living things, mankind has been blessed with a RUACH, which literally means wind or breath, and refers to our basic life-force or vital spirit. It is the invisible breath of God that animates physical human beings and it refers to the moral and emotional dimensions of our life and our ability to express human feelings and distinctive personal qualities, in speech, song and action. An occasion or a celebration is said to be blessed with a "good *ruach*" if the gathering has good spiritual vibrations and is pervaded by a wholesome atmosphere which is emotionally satisfying. It is God's *ruach* which revived the dry bones of Israel, as described in the Book of Ezekiel.

Finally, say the Rabbis, every man and woman has been blessed with a unique soul, *NESHAMAH*, which relates to our spirituality, intellect and power of thought. This is what gives us our precious capacity for understanding and curiosity. The Book of Genesis (chapter 2, verse 7) says that God formed Man out of the ground and breathed into his nostrils a soul, a breath of life. The Jewish belief is in life after death and in the immortality of the soul. Ecclesiastes, chapter 12, verse 7, says that, upon death, "the dust returns to the ground where it had been and the soul returns to God who had given it." A person is said to have a "good *NESHAMAH*" if he or she is pulled towards God, and if he or she displays desirable qualities such as humility, mercy, charity, piety and the will to follow the commandments of the Almighty.

The classic Jewish understanding is that a person's *LEV* (the heart) is the seat of his will. The prophet Ezekiel (chapter 11, verse 19) refers to the Jewish people's "heart of stone" which needed to change so that they could become responsive to God's will.

The Jewish holy writings, the *TANACH* (comprising mainly the Torah, the Prophets, the Psalms and the Talmud) contain three types of *MITZVOTH* (commandments). The first category of commandments is *CHUKIM*, where there is no obvious or compelling reason or explanation given for the performance of these *MITZVOTH*. Examples of these are the laws relating to eating *KOSHER* food and the special requirements concerning *PARAH ADUMAH* (red heifer). The second type of commandment comprises *MISHPATIM*, where there is an easy and obvious explanation for their strict observance, an obvious example being the prohibition against murder. Finally, we have *EDOT*, which are designed to remind us of the historical nature and the importance of the High Holidays, and the festivals, such as the Passover.

It would be fair to say that, during the past two millennia, the Torah, incorporating the Ten Commandments and an abundance of moral principles, has had a fundamental worldwide influence upon the conduct of society, both Jewish and Gentile.

However, as Jews have historically remained aloof from the proselytising process, it was left to Judaism's daughter religions, Christianity and Islam, to diffuse the principles of monotheism, morality and the importance of ethical behaviour throughout the world.

In the centuries after Moses received the Torah on Mount Sinai King Solomon built a Temple in Jerusalem and the Jewish religion began to be established. A succession of Hebrew prophets and sages began to make pronouncements and issue warnings against the perceived shortcomings of the rulers. They spoke truth and justice to authority and they pointed out that those in power did not have a monopoly of wisdom. Over time a set of beliefs and detailed practices were developed in order to clarify and explain the words of the Torah.

As indicated above, the Jewish journey began in a pagan world, where infanticide was widespread, where might was right and where the masses were kept illiterate and beholden to a ruling class. In a world of primitive biological instincts and animalistic appetites, there was little attempt to care for the weak or the sick; the mindset of the people could not accommodate such modern neighbourly concepts as charity and the care for the widow and orphan.

It took some time for the development of any kind of morality or discipline, both of which were necessary to rein in excessive or harsh demands by the upper echelons of the community. With Abraham and Moses there came advanced human values, such as a universal right to a peaceful and productive life, justice for all irrespective of wealth or status, good neighbourliness and, most important of all, the idea of bringing Heaven down to earth – in other words, the need to practice on earth the superior ideals and virtues which were deemed God-like.

Jews believe that an action will be judged "good" or "bad" when it is measured against an incorruptible, unbiased, moral code and unchanging ethics which are not influenced by any fashionable and capricious short-lived ideas blowing hither and thither. The "Western" concepts of right and wrong, which we take for granted today, together with all the sophisticated paraphernalia of acceptable conduct, have been honed and shaped on the anvil of religion, incorporating principles which had their origins in our biblical heritage.

The Jewish way of life is described as to its conduct, rather than to any propositions of belief or creed. Philosophy is not a term recognised in the Talmud. However, the great medieval Rabbi and physician, Maimonides, did compile a list known as the Thirteen Articles of Faith. They all start with the phrase *ANI MA-AMIN* (I believe with perfect faith). But, far more important than reciting a catechism is the need for the right action. Men and women are judged according to their ethical conduct, their prayers and their celebrations of festivals. The maxim that has come down through the ages is *NA'ASEI VE-NISHMA'A*, which, in relation to religious duties, can be very loosely and volubly translated as "We shall obey and we shall carry out, and in this way we will learn."

CHAPTER 6

Creation/Evolution: The Biblical Account

"Now we see how the astronomical evidence leads to a biblical view of the origin of the world. The astronomical and biblical accounts of Genesis are the same: the chain of events leading to man commenced suddenly and sharply at a definite moment in time."

Dr. Robert Jastrow, astrophysicist, *"God and the Astronomers"*

Our tradition tells us that, some 3,300 years ago, during the unprecedented march of freedom which the Israelites undertook after their many years of Egyptian servitude, God communicated to the world a most profound "charter," the Torah, which was intended to serve as the basis for the relationship between the Almighty and humankind. It is the foundation stone upon which the ethical and moral conduct of all humanity was intended to be built.

As leader of the Israelites, Moses was instructed to go up Mount Sinai in order to receive what we now call "the five Books of Moses." The mountain-side was miraculously covered in flowers and greenery for the occasion and, after communing with the Almighty for forty days and nights, Moses came down with the 2 stone tablets of the law (the Ten Commandments) together with the inspiration which led to the eventual compilation of the holy words of the Bible in its entirety. Just seven weeks previously the huge multitude of Israelites (previously known as Hebrews, later to be known as Jews to this very day) had been released from 210 years of slavery in Egypt. Well over two million people are believed to have heard the words spoken by God, and that momentous event still resonates with us today.

Apart from a broad historical overview and a narrative, the Torah incorporates precious revelations and a set of ethical principles and commandments which have been absorbed, consciously or otherwise, by vast swathes of humanity for more than two thousand years. Several quotations and extracts from the Torah have infiltrated into our common everyday language over the centuries. Many biblical expressions and turns of phrase are so much part of our culture that we barely recognise their origin. The actual words, the ethics and the laws revealed in the Torah have inspired the sentiments which have been expressed in the written constitution of some nation states and we can find echoes of relevant biblical expressions carved on public monuments and inscribed on important documents. We hardly need reminding that the Bible has been translated into more than a thousand languages and it still features near the top of the best-seller lists of books sold worldwide, year after year.

The Torah was originally transmitted by word of mouth through several generations of elders, sages and prophets, until about 2,500 years ago, when the Five Books were committed to writing for the first time. The Torah validates the continued existence of the Jews as "the People of the Book." The German poet Heinrich Heine has correctly described it as the portable homeland of the Jewish people.

Today, Orthodox Jewish congregations throughout the world hear relevant passages of the Torah chanted in time-hallowed manner, on Sabbaths, Festivals and High Holy Days. The Torah, together with the prophetic writings and the Psalms, became the major authority for the development of the Christian religion some hundreds of years later. Passages from the Torah as well as the pronouncements of the Jewish prophets are, in fact, read out aloud and commented on in the churches of most Christian denominations to this very day. Judaism's other daughter religion, Islam, acknowledges the relevance of some Biblical personalities (Adam, Abraham, Elijah and Moses), and Islamic liturgy makes reference to some events depicted therein, e.g. the binding by Abraham of his son on the sacrificial altar (although Islamic tradition refers to Ishmael, born to Hagar, rather than to Isaac, born to Sarah.)

It may appear that the Torah was originally written in a language designed to be easily understood by its first audience, but there are many subtleties, hidden allegories and pithy expressions which require careful elucidation.

The Five Books of Moses are:

BERESHEET (Genesis);

SHEMOT (Exodus);

VAYIKRA (Leviticus);

BAMIDBAR (Numbers); and

DEVARIM (Deuteronomy).

The printed version of the Torah is known as the *CHUMASH* (from the Hebrew root word, *CHAMISHAH*, meaning five); the Christians have bundled together the Torah, the Psalms, as well as the Prophetic writings and they have labelled them "The Old Testament." If you refer to the first of the five Books (Genesis, chapter 1, verses 1 to 5) you will find the following:

"In the beginning God created the heaven and the earth. Now the earth was unformed and void, and darkness was upon the face of the deep; and the spirit of God hovered over the face of the waters. And God said: "Let there be light," and there was light. And God saw the light, that it was good; and God divided the light from the darkness. And God called the light Day, and the darkness He called Night. And there was evening and there was morning, one day."

It is important to note that, according to the Bible, the first thing which was created was LIGHT – in Hebrew the word is *ORR*. There is a fairly close parallel here with the scientific narrative. Today the scientists are able to confirm that there had, indeed, been a particular and unique moment of creation, a huge, cataclysmic "Big Bang" event as the Universe exploded into being. And, if you go through the first few verses of the Bible, you will find some remarkable parallels between the narrative of creation as set out in the Torah and what the scientists have been telling us over the past few hundred years.

The words of the Bible make no attempt at indicating precisely when creation occurred. While the narrative refers to some unspecified time in the past, some Christian theologians have attempted to arrive at precise dates by using whatever clues are available in the text. In the seventeenth century Bishop Ussher, primate of all Ireland, came to the conclusion that the world was created on 27th October 4004 BCE, at precisely 9 in the morning. This attempt at precision is not something which Jewish theologians are interested to pursue.

Having announced the creation of the extraordinary light, the Torah then tells us that, on planet Earth, the heavens were separated from the waters below, and then the oceans and continents took shape. This was followed, on the third day, by the appearance of seed-bearing vegetation, grass and fruit-bearing trees.

There then follows a brief, non-scientific account of the natural progression in the creation process. We are told that, on the fourth day, the sun, the moon and the stars made their appearance. However, this part of the biblical narrative is contradicted by the scientific discoveries: we now know that, in fact, planet Earth made its appearance about 90 million years *after* the sun. On the fifth day, says the biblical narrative, the oceans began swarming with all manner of fish and sea creatures, and also on the same day, all manner of winged creatures flew overhead.

Creation of Humankind

Finally, on the sixth day, after all the creeping things and after all the four-legged animals appeared on Earth, God created the first man, Adam, and then the first woman, Eve.

Dr. J. H. Hertz, who was the British Chief Rabbi just before the Second World War, was the editor of the notes incorporated into the edition of the *HERTZ CHUMASH*. He says that the first few verses of Genesis represent:

"... a majestic summary of the story of creation: God is the beginning, nay, the Cause of all things. ... Ages untold may have elapsed between the calling of matter into being and the reduction of chaos to ordered arrangement."

Just 34 verses (434 Hebrew words) were needed to cover the whole creation narrative. Two pertinent questions arise here: Why was such an economy of words used to describe such an unprecedented event as the initial creation of the whole Universe? Why is there an absence of elaboration of the details of the events leading to the appearance of all the different life forms, and of mankind in particular?

The answer to both questions is this: The Torah does not purport to be a science text-book. If you want to delve into the "how" and "what" of the creative process you need to refer to tomes on astronomy, biology, chemistry, geology, palaeontology and physics. Science describes physical processes, whereas the Torah was designed to provide a basis for the inculcation of ethical belief and as a guide for personal conduct, not scientific enquiry. Rabbi Dr. Hertz provides a further illumination in his explanatory notes to Genesis:

"... When neighbouring peoples deified the sun, moon and stars, or worshipped ... the very beetles that crawled along its banks, the opening page of Scripture proclaimed in language of majestic simplicity that the universe and all ... therein ... are the product of one supreme directing Intelligence... an eternal, spiritual Being."

As already stated, the Torah appears to be totally silent as to the physical details of the creation process. All we are told is that creation happened as the result of God's decision and the whole process emanated from His word. It is also noticeable that there is no direct reference to the gradual evolution of species, culminating in the appearance of mankind. This has prompted many commentaries by our prophets, sages and Rabbis over the centuries.

The first chapter of Genesis expresses the account of creation in language which makes an immediate dramatic impact but Maimonides, the great Rabbi and physician, who strode the medieval world like a colossus, has stated that the account of creation given in the Scripture is not intended to be taken literally. In order to appreciate the full meaning of the Torah, including the disclosure of potentially hidden insights and obscure passages, you must have regard to the Talmud and the various commentaries of the sages. In ancient times, both in Judaism and Christianity, instruction was often conveyed poetically or allegorically, in ways which were designed to teach an important lesson in an interesting way. And so it is as regards certain sections of the Torah. The end of the creation account (Genesis, chapter 2, verses 1 to 3) reads as follows:

"And the heaven and the earth were finished ... And on the seventh day God finished His work which He had made; and He rested on the seventh day ... and God blessed the seventh day, and hallowed it."

The important question that now arises is this: what is the religious attitude towards the emphatically clear scientific assertion that, over the past 3.5 billion years or more, there has been a continuous process of evolution of the species, with forms of life first making an appearance in their most simple and primitive form, after which they began evolving incrementally, until today we see around us millions of different life forms, all possessing features of prodigious complexity? Is there an unresolved conflict between the biblical and the scientific account of creation and evolution?

The truth is that most modern Orthodox, and Reform Jews, as well as most Christians, do not feel challenged by the findings of science relating to the evolution process. It may come as a surprise to some people to learn that nearly all modern religious authorities have acknowledged that there is nothing sacrilegious in the concept of evolution or mutation, from the simple to the complex, from the lowest to the highest, it being clearly understood that the steps in the progression are all acts of Divine will.

The belief today is that the creation of the genome has inevitably introduced the possibility of copying errors. Scientists may describe evolution as a "blind process". There is no doubt, however, that these tiny "rogue" interventions have resulted in an evolving bio-diversity which has ultimately led to the evolution of humankind.

The Bible itself hints at the general truth of evolution by referring to the transition from the chaos that existed before creation to the order that followed it. The mutation or evolution of species, from the simple to the most complex, from the lowest to the highest, is fully in accordance with Jewish (and Christian) understanding of the will of God. Some commentators have pointed out that the biblical account hints at the need for the evolutionary process to continue after the initial act of creation of the Almighty. This is because the very last four Hebrew words of Genesis, chapter 2 verse 3, read as follows:

"... ASHER BARAH ELOKIM LA-ASOT"

The word *BARAH* comes from the Hebrew verb "to create," whereas *LA-ASOT* comes from the verb "to make." Our sages say that it is only God who can create – He brought forth the Universe as well as the primitive life-forms *ex nihilo*, out of absolutely nothing – whereas mankind only "makes," i.e., as mortals, we are only capable of producing something using materials and resources already made available around us. Our sages and commentators have taught us that the verse quoted above offers a tantalising clue as to God's real intentions. There is a strong implication in that phrase and, particularly by the use of the apparently superfluous words "to make," that, after the initial Divine creation of the world, it was left to the natural processes of evolution and adaptation to develop species and features as needed, aided where necessary by the actions of mankind. In truth, therefore, having made the statement announcing the initial creation, the Torah is singularly uninterested in the *minutiae* of the evolution process, the mechanism by which life was formed and developed.

In the past some people may have had a problem with understanding the word "day" as used in the creation narrative. Bear in mind that the Bible is not a scientific textbook, and it does not always employ language in a dry and precise way. Making due allowances for the fact that religious teachers, both ancient and modern, have often expressed themselves in parables, we can confidently state that the expression "day" and the phrase "there was evening and there was morning" must be taken to signify a poetic expression of a non-specific period of time, perhaps comprising millions or even billions of years.

Regarding the age of the Universe, here once again there is little dispute among most of the modern Jewish and Christian theologians that the opening chapter of the Torah could not be read literally. Adam and Eve were never intended to be seen as historical figures.

In summary, then, we can say that most adherents of all the main world faiths, have no difficulty in accepting that, having created the Universe, God then put in place the necessary initial conditions for the formation of all the planetary bodies, all the essential physical constants, the subtle laws of nature, the self-replicating living cells, and all other conditions for the continued evolution and the magnificent profusion of life on planet Earth.

Furthermore, apart from a small minority of distinguished men and women who believe otherwise, the rest of us have no difficulty in believing that God chose the route of evolution and natural selection which, coupled with the granting to man of the important attribute of free will, has resulted in the creation of conditions for the fulfilment of His Divine purposes. We believe that it was God's desire that men and women should be created to be "the goal and crown of creation," endowed with rational and moral faculties and capable of high ethical and spiritual attainment, and He provided the means for the achievement of His wishes.

In 2014 the Ministry of Education in Britain decided that the scientific theory of the evolution of the species, as originally propounded by Charles Darwin, should, for the first time, be taught in British primary schools. It is well known, however, from research in schools in USA, that the core Darwinian ideas of "adaptation" and "natural selection" are rather difficult concepts to teach young children of 10 and 11 years of age, particularly those of a deeply religious background, who believe in the literal words of the Bible.

Coincidentally, the Israeli Ministry of Education also announced in recent months that Darwin's Theory of Evolution will be taught throughout the nation's school system, including those run on strictly religious lines. This decision may appear, at first sight, to be a reversal in Jewish religious faith, maybe a change of heart on the part of the Jewish religious establishment, but, in reality, it follows on from the generally accepted belief that:

1. People do not derive scientific education from the Torah and, in any case, the Bible can only be fully understood after consulting the commentaries which have appeared over the past 2,500 years.

2. We have taken on board the scientific discoveries made over the past several centuries. Most theological

commentators accept that the Universe was created billions of years ago and the various forms of life have been evolving ever since. The six days of creation mentioned in the Bible must be understood in conceptual rather than in historical terms. The scientific explanations for the evolution of the several species leading to mankind have no specific religious significance.

3. During the past one hundred years several prominent Rabbis, such as Rav Kook, the first Ashkenazi Chief Rabbi of the Holy Land, and Rabbi Samson Raphael Hirsch, have expressed no theological reservations in accepting Darwin's main thesis. The teachings of our modern and forward-looking Rabbis is that God has blessed the Earth with the need and the wherewithal for the creation of an astounding diversity of life forms, all of which have undergone a process of biological evolution and adjustment to conditions on our planet. We accept that, from a single amorphous nucleus and a single law of adaptation and heredity, He has created order out of chaos and He has willed the whole of creation.

4. We know that, as regards our physical attributes, men and women have much in common with many mammalian species. Where we differ is in humanity's unique soul, our *NESHAMAH*. Over a period of hundreds of thousands of generations, spanning millions of years, we have been able to rise well above most of our animalistic origins and crude instincts.

CHAPTER 7

The God Dimension

"God is He than whom nothing greater can be conceived."

Saadiah Gaon, Rabbi and philosopher (died 942 CE)

Vast swathes of mankind have, for thousands of years, harboured a strong feeling that there exists a Being, a Superhuman Intelligence, an unseen Power, to whom we need to express our devotion. The conviction among believers is that the unseen Presence, whom we call God, is "that beyond which there is no other," incorporeal and indescribable in human terms, but who, nevertheless, urges us to achieve ever-higher levels of perfection. Although we, as believers, stand in awe of His powers, we will never be able to prove His existence in the way one can prove the "truth" of a piece of Euclidean geometry.

The Book of Exodus (chapter 33, verse 11) says that "The Lord spoke unto Moses *PANIM-EL-PANIM* (face-to-face), as a man speaketh unto his friend." However, the plain fact is that no human being has actually seen God. When Moses says to God,

"Show me, I pray Thee, Thy glory", the answer is loud and clear: "Thou canst not see My face, for man shall not see Me and live." Jewish people have always been extremely reluctant to discuss God's physical features or attributes for the simple reason that we would not be comfortable in ascribing any anthropomorphic characteristics to The Almighty. Of course, the Torah makes reference to conversations which God did have, from time to time, with leading Biblical personalities, such as Moses, Aaron and Elijah.

The biblical story of the Tower of Babel emphasises the fact that mankind's relationship with God is couched in ethical and emotional terms, but we are not empowered to delve too deeply into His mystery. The story, which has apocryphal overtones, is set in Shinar, near the Euphrates River, many years after the episode of Noah and the Flood, but before the time of Abraham. The people began to settle on the land and they all spoke the same language.

The people's pride in their material achievements led them to show conceit and disrespect towards God. In an act of hubristic defiance, using their new-found skills in brick-making and the use of bitumen, they decided to construct a tall tower with the intention of reaching the heavens. This ill-considered attempt at physically climbing up the huge tower in order to fulfil their desire to see God ended in disaster. There was a serious chaotic situation, the tower was partially destroyed, mankind henceforth spoke in many tongues and they were dispersed unto all four corners of the globe. The lesson to be learnt from this story is that some matters relate to God alone and mankind cannot presume to understand everything about Him.

Of course, we know about God from several sources: from a direct reading of the Bible, from studying the pronouncements of the Prophets, from poring over the extensive rabbinical commentaries and, most of all, from acknowledging what He has done for us. It is a fundamental Jewish belief that God has connected with mankind in three ways: **Creation, Revelation** and **Redemption**. In other words, God has, firstly, illustrated His superhuman powers by creating the whole Universe. Our allegiance is then buttressed by revelation (He granted us the Torah) and by deed (He redeemed our ancestors from Egyptian slavery). We also believe that in more recent times He has been instrumental in the rebirth of the state of Israel in our days leading to the ingathering of millions of exiles to our Holy Land. In other words, God is very much part of the world's past, present and future, as demonstrated in His majestic statement: *EHYEH ASHER EHYEH*. This is often translated as "I am what I am," but a better interpretation would be "I shall be what I choose to be."

Perhaps the one word which encapsulates for mankind the nature of the Almighty is the word *CHESED* (see Exodus, chapter 34, verses 6 and 7). The English language has struggled to find the correct translation of this word and has come up with "loving-kindness" which goes most of the way to conveying the meaning of the word. The Hebrew word includes other precious qualities: loyalty, faithfulness, mercy and a covenantal promise to maintain a relationship with mankind even when the recipient of that *CHESED* is unworthy of such love and concern.

God is known through the loving-kindness which is shown to us, through His ever-present support, assistance and mercy to us at crucial moments. Our prayers make constant reference to what are termed "the thirteen characteristics of the Divine Nature." The Book of Exodus (chapter 34, verses 6 and 7) reads partly as follows:

> *"..... The Lord God, merciful and gracious, long-suffering, and abundant in goodness and truth; keeping mercy unto the thousandth generation, forgiving iniquity and transgression and sin ..."*

Throughout our liturgy we are urged to serve God "with all your heart, with all your soul and all your might." We are also encouraged to imitate Him (*imitatio Dei*) but, of course, there is a limit on mortal man's ability in that regard.

We know in our hearts and in our minds that God is infinite and omnipresent. Although mankind is, of course, denied those two Divine qualities we can try to put into practice His other characteristics: we can be merciful and compassionate and we can attempt to live in ways that are in accordance with His *MITZVOTH* (commandments). We aspire to imitate God because, to quote from the Book of Leviticus, we are urged to "be holy because I, the Lord your God, am holy." There is, for example, an important requirement to bury the dead (as God buried Moses) and we are urged to visit the sick (as God visited Abraham when he was unwell).

The Power of Prayer

The first few pages of the Jewish Book of Prayer are headed "On Waking" and the subsequent pages include prayers for other occasions. All prayers are directed to the Almighty, and they usually include supplications for forgiveness and expressions of perfect faith in the Creator. Other prayers make reference to Jewish history (e.g. our deliverance from slavery in Egypt), we express our sense of profound sorrow that our Holy Temple in Jerusalem is no more, and we entertain the hope that the Messiah will come speedily in our days.

Numerous prayers are specifically designed to be recited at home, such as the prayers to be recited before and after the partaking of any food, before lighting the Sabbath candles and before retiring to bed at night. There is a significant component of prayers related to the festivals such as those related to the reading of the *HAGGADAH* during Pesach or the lighting of the special *MENORAH* during the eight days of *CHANUKAH*, the festival of lights.

People of a religious disposition have a desire to hold a dialogue with God on a regular basis. The Hebrew word for prayer is *TEFILLAH* and it implies an act of self-judgment, a spontaneous outpouring of the human heart. Through dint of the regular repetition of formulaic words and sacred chanting we are reinforcing our sacred beliefs. This regular communing with the Almighty is usually carried out in the presence of a congregation, although there are many occasions when we find ourselves in circumstances when we need to pray on our own. Prayer has the effect of helping us to concentrate and synthesise our thoughts on the important things in life, our family relations and the environment.

Prayer reminds us who we are, where we come from and it helps us to focus on our historical heritage and the direction of our lives. Prayer elevates us. It spells out life's truths, connects us to the great ideas that make life worth living and concentrates our attention on verities we would otherwise forget. It enhances the imprint that we wish to embed into the make-up of our personality. In prayer our hearts are opened, our minds soar heavenwards, we leave behind the mundane and we mentally shape ourselves into the personality that we wish to become.

Prayer is, ultimately, as exercise in self-improvement. It highlights the contrast between our puny self, measured against the heavenly ideal, and it pulls us up along the road we need to take in order to strive for perfection. There is a constant obligation to place our unwavering trust in the Almighty, to hold on to our belief that our prayers will eventually reach God and that He will make His responses in His own way and in His own time.

Of course, it is possible to live without prayer, without faith. But it is a life diminished and emotionally truncated. True, mankind prays to an invisible God, but to deny prayer is to deny the still, small voice within us, the voice of reason and discipline. There are some who say that they cannot see the point of reciting well-worn phrases, and they cannot understand how our prayers will change God's will. Surely, they maintain, whatever the Almighty has in store for us cannot be reversed. Those without faith assert that prayer implies that we entertain doubts about God's loving-kindness. Worse, they say, does it suggest that we are questioning His sense of compassion or justice? The proper response is that prayer expresses our frailty and inadequacy. Through prayer we hope to become more worthy of whatever it is that God has decided for us.

"Prayer does not change God, but it changes him who prays."

Soren Kierkegaard, Danish philosopher

In April 2015 there was an interesting and prominent report in *The Times* newspaper headed, *"Put to the test, even atheists believe in God."* This academic investigation, carried out in USA, Canada and Finland, found that whether people are religious or not, we all have a "naked intuition" that all natural objects which we see around us (e.g. volcanoes, giraffes, stalagmites, a tiger's paw) were, indeed, created by a higher power. The academics reported that "there was a deep-seated automatic tendency to see intentional causation in nature" among several hundred people, whether they were believers, atheists or agnostics. A similar survey is now planned to be held in China to see whether there exists a similar belief system in that vast country.

Will my Prayers be Answered?

It is a truism that, at some time in our lives, some of us will have found ourselves in a desperately difficult, dangerous or even a life-threatening situation which required strong immediate assistance, whether physical or emotional. At some time or another some of us may be sitting in a doctor's surgery, ashen-faced, because we have just been given an unbearably serious medical diagnosis. At other times, we may have to confront an apparently unsolvable relational or business situation. When we find ourselves in a tight spot with seemingly no escape, when we are confronted with an intractable problem, the natural reaction for many of us is to look up to the heavens and call upon God to extend a helping hand, whether we are believers or not.

However, it would be true to say that very few of us can say that our prayers have elicited an immediate favourable response from on high. So, the question is: How long must I wait for God to respond? Where is the evidence that God is listening? In the Book of Job (chapter 30, verse 20) we find the following heart-rending words, obviously spoken by somebody who is undergoing a series of trials and tribulations, physical and mental:

"I cry unto Thee and Thou dost not hear me; I stand up, and Thou regardest me not."

Our sages have come up with various responses in their attempt at helping us to grapple with these understandable cries from the heart. A partial answer can be found in Psalm 66, verse 18:

"If I regard iniquity in my heart, the Lord will not hear me."

In other words, God will deny our prayers until they are purged of all selfishness. Only those with clean hands and pure hearts can expect a response from the Lord.

At one point, when he was at the end of his tether, Job begged God to take his life away, but, of course, we cannot expect such a prayer to be given a favourable response.

Neither can we expect any response from God if our prayer includes the random venting of silly notions or if we were to express a need for revenge or if we display evidence of petty jealousies.

The ceiling of the Sistine Chapel in the Vatican depicts God as an old and venerable man, in a long beard, seated in a comfortable armchair. This does not conform to the Jewish idea of the Almighty. Some people may regard God as a rich and indulgent uncle, somebody in possession of a store of goodies which are ready to be dispensed to any supplicant who asks, irrespective of need. That is not going to happen. It is up to us, the hopeful recipients of heavenly favours, to be pro-active. We make a grave mistake if we think that, faced with a particular need or placed in a difficult situation, all it takes is for us to submit our request, as if a take-away service was in operation, and then we can just sit back, while the necessary ingredients are assembled and get processed in some heavenly workshop or laboratory, before the finished product, the perfect answer to our prayer, rolls down in our direction. It does not work that way. God expects some positive action from us before we may be deemed to be worthy recipients of heavenly favours. We cannot just wait for things to happen miraculously and we cannot expect a heavenly response which will fully meet our needs precisely.

Our forefather Abraham and his wife Sarah were childless for the greater part of their lives. Their daily prayers, their heartfelt longing to be initiated into the joys of parenthood, did not elicit a response until they were near the end of their lives. Abraham was in his nineties when he became the father to Ishmael, his first son, as a result of his relationship with Sarah's handmaiden, Hagar. Later he had a second son, Isaac, whose mother was Sarah. Subsequently, God promised Abraham that his "seed shall multiply" and, eventually, he will be "the father of a great nation." From this we learn that the longer we have to wait for the answer to our prayer, the more perfect the answer may well be in the end. We also learn that God chooses to answer our prayers in His own way and He can never be rushed.

An obvious point to make is that you cannot say that God is apparently not listening to your prayers if you, for your part, are not in regular conversation with Him and you only come to Him in times of distress and need. Also, it is important to understand that God's agenda and plans are not the same as ours and, of course, His time-scale is completely different. The true believer will leave the shaping of God's answer to His mercy and he or she will welcome whatever response they receive in due course.

During the festival of *SUKKOT* (the autumnal feast of Tabernacles) we pray to the Almighty expressing hope that the Holy Land will be blessed with plentiful rain, in due time, so that the farms and agricultural settlements will enjoy a successful and productive growing season. We are not asking that the natural celestial order be suspended in order to suit our particular convenience. That is the wrong motivation. Prayer is the conduit which, in this instance, affords us the opportunity to contemplate on the many wonders of our living environment and we are made aware of the need not to waste or despoil our precious natural resources, of which water is such a vital part.

Likewise, when we learn that ill-health has caused somebody we know, whether close relative or dear friend, to be bed-ridden or having to undergo prolonged treatment for a serious medical condition, it is customary to pronounce the words *REFUAH SHELEMAH* (we express the hope that he/she may be speedily restored to good health, in mind and body). Whether praying alone or as a member of a congregation, what we are really doing here is spending a few moments to appreciate the qualities of the person who is unwell. We reflect on our bond of kinship or friendship and we may even be prompted to see what we can do, by way of a kind word or gesture, to alleviate any physical pain or lessen their mental burden.

It is true that, during the time of the founders of our religion, miraculous events did take place, such as the parting of the Red Sea (or the Sea of Reeds as it should be called) or the provision of *MANNA* during the time when our people were sojourning for 40 years on their way to the Promised Land. Much later, Scripture records that, in the ninth century BCE, the Hebrew prophet Elijah needed to challenge King Ahab in order to eliminate the practice of worshiping the pagan god Baal. Two altars were erected, one to the false pagan gods and one to Yahweh. After all the incantations of the hundreds of pagan priests, which were addressed to Baal, proved to be completely unproductive, Elijah stepped forward. He prayed to the Almighty and a fire came down immediately from heaven, causing his sacrifice to be consumed in the proper way.

However, Maimonides taught us not to rely on similar spectacular miracles today. We cannot expect a direct response from Heaven. It is important to remember that these miracles, where something happens which is totally unexpected and out of the ordinary, they were not meant to be seen as a conjurer's illusion, to be enjoyed as entertainment. They were not designed merely to ensure the people's continued loyalty to the Almighty who possessed these extraordinary powers. The miraculous events took place at a specific time in order to solve a critical and urgent need. Rather than waiting and longing for extraordinary miracles to happen, we ought to be realists and we ought to be celebrating the pervading natural laws, giving thanks for the safety and comfort we all derive from the order and regularity which exists in the natural world.

The first Prime Minister of modern Israel, David Ben-Gurion was once asked whether he believed in miracles. He answered, "In Israel, in order to be a realist you *must* believe in miracles."

CHAPTER 8

Spirituality, Religion, Morality

"Everyone who is seriously involved in the pursuit of science becomes convinced that a spirit is manifest in the laws of the Universe – a spirit vastly superior to that of man, and one in the face of which we, with our modest powers, must feel humble."

Albert Einstein, physics Nobel Laureate

It would be useful, at this stage, to attempt some explanations. We need to arrive at workable definitions of the words "spirituality", "religion" and "morality" and see how they are interrelated.

Spirituality is an intensely powerful personal feeling, a natural state of mind which draws a person away from the mundane present and on to a higher, mysterious plane. It is a feeling that makes us connected to a non-human, elemental power, even though we are unable to prove the existence or the origin of that power.

During the year 2014 many countries marked the centenary of the start of the First World War. One of the most poignant and spiritually satisfying events during the summer and early autumn of the centenary year was the "planting" of more than 800,000 ceramic poppies in the moat surrounding the Tower of London, one for each British and Commonwealth life sadly lost in the field of battle. There was an outpouring of sympathy, an act of collective remembrance, honouring those who had given their lives in the defence of the country. For the 5 million people who visited and gazed at the impressive display of blood-red flowers there was an opportunity to reflect on the nature of war as well as on the physical and emotional damage it can leave in its wake. Many shed tears as they remembered some long-dead relative or ancestral friend, most of whom were struck down in the prime of their lives.

Undoubtedly, the British people, whether they belonged to one or other religious group or, indeed, even if they had no personal religious affiliation, experienced a few moments of compassion and grief. The sadness, the emotional connection, the moments of reflection, and the respect shown to the departed are all different manifestations of our exclusively human spirituality.

From time to time most people will have experienced similar moments of transcendence. When you are listening to a particular piece of familiar uplifting music, or attending the celebration of an important family event, or when you are walking with your daughter down the aisle on her wedding day, all of these moments must surely induce a feeling that you are connected to a different, ethereal, world. Spiritual moments such as these can be wholesome and nourishing; they can be uplifting, therapeutic and calming.

During moments of stillness we may be tempted to reminisce or to contemplate on the totality of our lives, when these intensely personal experiences are said to "touch our soul." We may be overcome by palpable emotional feelings of pure joy and happiness, or, depending on one's age and state of health, however, some of us may be tempted to consider what happens when, eventually, we will reach the end of our natural lives. These spiritual feelings are intensified for people who are seriously ill and about to undergo a major medical procedure. Equally, we can imagine that soldiers on combat duty, just before undertaking a potentially dangerous mission, will surely experience a feeling that they are alone and vulnerable and they need to call upon a higher power to their aid.

In 1967, when the Israeli forces, having overcome seemingly insuperable military odds, finally achieved a breakthrough and arrived at the Western Wall in Jerusalem, there were unforgettable spiritual moments of euphoria when the SHOFAR (the ram's horn) was sounded in the moment of victory. The Chief of Staff, General Yitzhak Rabin, a dour man not normally given to expressions of spirituality, recorded his thoughts:

"The overwhelming desire was to cling to the Wall, to hold on to that great moment as long as possible."

Our human ancestors who lived 40,000 years ago almost certainly had spiritual feelings and they expressed some of them by etching and painting on the cave walls or by creating crude fertility deities out of stone.

Some anthropologists have speculated that the representation of animals, geometric patterns and hand shapes, incised or painted on the walls of caves, may be the manifestation of an embryonic religious dimension, a non-physical, spiritual relationship which needed to be expressed.

The fact that today, all over the world, many people (even those who are not connected at all to a specific religion) feel the need to demonstrate an allegiance to some higher power or some unknown spirits is a pretty strong indication that spirituality is hard-wired into our genes (I doubt, however, that there is anything like a unique "spirituality-gene"!). Humans feel instinctively impelled, for example, to show compassion and empathy towards other sentient beings, both human and animal, we take time to admire beautiful objects and geographical features and we try not to despoil the environment that is all around us. Of course, being akin to mysticism, these feelings of spirituality are not literally provable, nor can they be dissected or examined in a laboratory. But nobody can deny that spirituality is a distinguishing feature in the make-up of *Homo sapiens,* and it is an attribute which is not replicated in other animals.

Spirituality, which speaks of an attachment to broad concepts such as hope, mercy, beauty, justice, empathy and compassion may or may not be transmuted into a specific and detailed religious way of life.

Religion encompasses the attachment to a set of beliefs, disciplines and character-forming practices directed to the worship of God. It is the formalisation of the many values which puts into practice the spiritual yearnings of like-minded individuals. Whereas spirituality comes naturally, good religious behaviour requires effort, commitment and practice. Whereas spirituality is intensely personal, religion is institutional.

Adherents of all faiths know that religious practice provides a necessary structure and discipline in their lives and it serves as a conduit for community action. It generates goodwill, fellow-feeling and warm camaraderie. Religion encourages feelings of repose, comfort and acceptance when faced with adversity and it may make our contemplation of death more tolerable.

Religion facilitates the nurturing of interlocking beliefs, sets of values and practices which, taken together and acted upon with sincerity, has a salutary effect. Imagine a bucolic scene, with young children enjoying themselves in the May sunshine, some holding a colourful ribbon attached to a central pole. By themselves, each young person cannot achieve very much. But, when a dozen or so children, each with a ribbon in their hand, all move in a graceful pattern round the pole, the interlocking colourful ribbons are woven together, thus creating something which is a joy to behold. And so it is when a group of people meet for worship in a house of prayer – a bonding of like-minded people is achieved.

Religion would make no sense if it fails to bring together people of similar beliefs who wish to work in tandem to promote comradeship and community activities.

Formal religious beliefs and practices have evolved and developed gradually over the last several thousand years and they were deemed necessary to mark the conversion of innate spiritual feelings into something that can be celebrated and commemorated in prayer, in the company of people of the same faith. It is the mortar that creates communal cohesion through the observance of prescribed rituals, the celebration of note-worthy historical events, the compliance with any dietary laws and the channelling of charitable endeavours. Very importantly, religious adherents feel grounded in the knowledge that they belong to a community of people, outside their immediate family circle, each acknowledging and celebrating their joint inherited culture. I have visited places of worship in Canberra, Rome, Harare and Jerusalem and I have enjoyed being welcomed and made to feel at home as a member of a warm spiritual fraternity which spans the globe. It is all about identity and the need to preserve precious historical traditions from one generation to the next.

The true religious experience is the attempt at elevating mankind to strive towards ever-higher levels of ethical behaviour, in order to live up to our belief that we are made "in the image of God." Religion explores the relationship between earthly man and a superhuman Creator, and touches upon the mysteries of human existence. It asks questions about human conduct and suggests ways of handling relationships with our extended family or with other members of the community.

The Bible and the various prophets give guidance as to the broad objectives of mankind in everyday life. For example, Deuteronomy (chapter 16, verse 20) says, "Justice, justice, shall you pursue", and the prophet Micah (chapter 6, Verse 8) says:

"He has told you, O man, what is good and what God requires of you; only to do justice and to love mercy, and to walk humbly with your God."

Members of religious groups feel focused and secure when they spend a moment or two in conversation with The Almighty. They would feel bereft if they did not incorporate a religious component into their lives, and more especially so if they do not offer prayers on a regular basis.

If you believe that God is vested with a unique oneness and righteousness, and if you believe that His word is to be accepted and followed, then that will provide you with the courage, confidence and moral fibre to face any potential challenge or threat.

In ancient times religion was deemed to be part of "the establishment" and it was enshrined in the hierarchical nature of society. The masses were powerless and they wallowed in ignorance and servitude. In the centuries after Moses received the Torah on Mount Sinai there was a succession of Hebrew prophets and sages (Isaiah, Jeremiah, Ezekiel, Micah, etc.) who stood up to authority and spoke out against the perceived shortcomings of the rulers. During the first five centuries of the Common Era the comprehensive Babylonian Talmud, as well as the shorter Jerusalem Talmud, were completed and incorporated into Jewish canon law. They delved into and elucidated the hidden meaning of certain Bible passages and they also prescribed the minutiae of religious observance.

Religion, however, can be hijacked by those who are dogmatic or stubbornly refuse to see the alternative point of view. The internecine conflicts fuelled by religious differences and spurred by extremists have the effect of damaging the potentially amicable relationship which we should have for each other. Just as milk becomes curdled and undrinkable by a few drops of lemon juice, so the ethos of a whole community can get congealed and turn sour if a small band of people, imbued with excessive and misguided religious fervour, seek to achieve their objectives through extremist or criminal action.

But, while most of us seek comfort and satisfaction from paying homage to a deity, there is no doubt that there are millions of people, be they atheists or agnostics, who own up to hardly any religious feelings at all, nor do they bother with any kind of ritual observance. They seem to derive no satisfaction from taking part in any religious celebration or commemoration and they seldom, if ever, step into any house of prayer. However, Judaism is not a coercive religion, so people born into the faith do not lose their Jewish status merely on account of the fact that they may not be active participants in the religious minutiae on a day-to-day basis or if they feel somewhat detached from the Jewish mainstream. There is a powerful concept of *TESHUVAH*, repentance or return, which allows people to reclaim their Jewish heritage at any time in the future, should they so desire.

Morality is almost an overused word these days. Moral laws are an expression of mankind's attempt at differentiating between behaviour which is right and acceptable on the one hand and those which are wrong and unacceptable on the other. Morality speaks to our own individual conscience and it is popularly regarded as a collection of values, precepts and obligations which ought to be the default position when we are contemplating a new standard of behaviour or when we are asked to judge a particular action which is taking place within our community or within society at large. The word morality is sometimes used in conjunction with the word ethics. Ethics, however, defines the collective standard of morality expected of a group or association to which a person belongs. One can make reference, therefore, to journalistic ethics, legal ethics or medical ethics, etc., as the bench-mark or standard of behaviour below which an individual member of the relevant group is not expected to fall.

Over the years theologians and philosophers have been asking the following questions: where do the concepts of good and evil come from? Whence do we derive the judgment which leads us to believe that a particular action is "morally acceptable?"

Some people have speculated that we need to delve into the process of human evolution, over billions of years, in order to locate the source of morality. This is not a satisfactory answer because there are no such things as "moral" atoms or cells or genes. The process of the evolution of mankind makes no distinction between "accepted" and "acceptable" behaviour.

It is pretty obvious that nature is not cruel; rather, it is pitilessly indifferent. Nature does not care about morals. Things happen in nature without the need to agonise over the most "moral" or "right" course of action. If nothing in nature has intrinsically moral consequences the next question is this: "how should we choose to behave?" The difficulty is that sometimes the choice is between a greater or lesser evil. Centuries ago infanticide and the deliberate killing of people as human sacrifices to propitiate a perceived deity or sun-god were considered morally accept-able. The belief then was that such actions would ensure the arrival of plentiful rains in due time, something which was beneficial to society at large. Human sacrifice (the killing of a certain number of people in order to avoid general famine in the future) was accepted then but it is certainly not acceptable today. In effect, the goalposts have been moved, and they have continued to move over the centuries.

One would like to believe that, within the make-up of every human, there is a deep sense of justice and fairness and a desire to do the right thing. When lawyers refer to "natural law" they are actually referring to moral proclivities such as these. Ulti-mately, these are values which are designed to achieve a good and fundamentally decent life for the majority. Moral laws, which are intended to lead to ethical and equitable behaviour, both individually and collectively, are fundamentally opposed to malevolence and they are intended to avoid the infliction of gratuitous pain and distress.

However, the question arises: do men and women always strive to do the right thing and always reject the wrong? The answer is that most theologians and people of faith would agree with the following proposition by Maimonides:

> "Every individual has a free choice ... every individual can be as righteous as Moses or as wicked as Jeroboam."

Many atheists, however, reject the idea of "human free will," whereas this concept is an integral part of religious belief. People of faith believe that, unless there are extenuating circumstances, a person does something wrong because he or she has wilfully and maliciously seen fit to do it. Criminals should not be able to plead "determinism" (i.e. that they are mere victims of internal powerful forces and circumstances which they are unable to control) in the hope of being exonerated from moral responsibility from any wrongdoing.

Could the source of morality be our inherent human nature or conscience? This can only be a partial answer because we believe that, from a very early age, humans are endowed with both good and evil inclinations. More importantly, because we have been invested with the faculty of free will, and because we behave in a manner of our own individual choosing, there is no possibility of anchoring morality in a universally accepted and acceptable standard of behaviour, free of evil, bias and distortion.

Over thousands of years there have been many examples of countries being ruled by deliberately ruthless demagogues who have imposed their thuggish policies by terror, the manipulation of the media or by some other means. For example, most of the people who came under the sway of the German Nazi regime before and during the Second World War were quite prepared to accept, without question, the need to inflict cruel genocidal action against millions of their fellow citizens. This totally vile and inhuman behaviour was justified and promoted on the grounds of "national unity," or the need to maintain racial purity or some other spurious premise, but it is very far from the acceptable conscience of humanity today.

Throughout the ages men and women have been prepared to take action which would be considered egocentric or unkind or ruthless. We therefore cannot say that morality is derived from human nature because too often our behaviour is motivated by greed and selfishness, with little regard given to those less fortunate or those more vulnerable in society.

Morality is not just a question of choosing between behaviour which "I like" and discarding those which "I don't like." Rather, morality distinguishes between "what is" and "what ought to be."

Morality cannot be rooted in science because you cannot describe ethics by reference to precise formulae. There is no biological route leading to ethical behaviour, no rational formula to help us discern right from wrong, and no scientific procedure that we can use to nourish our spirit of altruism and inspire our concern for others.

Moral laws would only pass the test of acceptability if we could point to some fixed impartial standard or bench-mark against which actions could be measured. One is inevitably drawn to the conclusion, therefore, that morality can only be derived from a source beyond man and outside nature. In other words, moral laws are derived from God. This does not mean, of course, that you have to belong to a religious order or fraternity in order to be moral. Most atheists behave in a perfectly acceptable moral way, just as there are thousands of religious people who are prepared to act in a morally reprehensible way.

There is a whole range of acceptable and wholesome moral actions. "Doing the right thing" includes such basic convictions that it is wrong to commit theft or murder, that one should refrain from telling a blatant lie and, of course, that we should altruistically offer our seat on a crowded bus to an old lady laden with heavy shopping parcels. True altruism implies that we are helping another person with no obvious hidden motive or expectation that a "good turn" will be reciprocated at some future time.

Some sceptics and scoffers are of the opinion that altruism is simply a manifestation of good reciprocal behaviour which mankind has devised in order to enable society to get on and progress. Of course, religion promotes the concept that "the right behaviour pays dividends." But we should reject the view, propounded by unbelievers, that morality and ethical principles were mere adaptations which have been foisted upon us by evolutionary mechanisms designed to maximise survival of our species. In other words, ethics is not an indication that genes have insinuated themselves upon us in order to enable us to secure our place in the evolutionary process and ensure mankind's reproductive advantage.

A society which is not characterised by moral righteousness is essentially flawed and will ultimately fail. The proof is demonstrated by the experience of people who have undoubtedly suffered under the unjust regime of the Russian Czars, the bestiality of the Nazi Third Reich and the ruthless and ungodly Communist regimes of the USSR, China and Cambodia. Thankfully, all these regimes, and all the evil that they represented, have been consigned to the dustbin of history, but there are more recent examples of regimes which are acting in an immoral or discriminatory way towards certain minority groups of their citizens.

It is pretty obvious that there is a stark contrast between the moral underpinning of human behaviour on the one hand and the behaviour of the wild animals on the African savannah on the other. A lioness with two fractious and hungry cubs in tow has no moral scruples. She has nothing to go on except her instincts. She leaves her cubs in a safe area, she goes on a hunting expedition and, if successful, she comes back with a freshly killed impala. The family can now tuck into some valuable nourishment and survive for another few days. If, a few months later, the lioness's original partner dies and she then hitches up with a new mate, the newly-installed alpha lion feels, instinctively, that he has to kill one or both of his new mate's cubs because he was not their biological father. He has no moral scruples about that either. His imperative is to push these cubs out of the way and to ensure that his own genes take priority in being passed on to the next generation.

Over the past several millennia men and women have been able to conquer the natural instincts which we originally

CHAPTER 8   SPIRITUALITY, RELIGION, MORALITY

inherited from our primitive animal ancestors and which would have led us to behave in the same way as other animals. Because we are blessed with a sophisticated brain, we are able to plan ahead. We herd cattle in farms to provide us with milk and beef. Slaughtering is done as humanely as possible. In this way we are able to rise above our need for instant gratification and we inflict minimum pain and suffering on the sentient animals which we use for food. In fact, nearly 15% of the British population have gone further – they have voluntarily embraced the concept of vegetarianism or veganism.

As regards the jealousy of a step-parent, that is certainly not how most of us humans behave. Millions of men and women all over the world have learnt to live with step-children, and we have long since extinguished any innate desire to carry out any harmful act towards them. Again, mankind has been able to reach a higher moral plane, something which the lesser animals are unable to do.

Because we now believe that all human beings are equal before God and in the eyes of the law, it was necessary to enshrine certain important moral principles of justice, equality and fairness in the Constitution of the United States and, later, some of the high-minded principles were incorporated into the United Nations Declaration of Human Rights. Article 18 of this latter document states, *inter alia*, that all persons are born free, they have the right to live in peace and harmony, they are equal before the law, and they are entitled to exercise their freedom of conscience and expression, as well as the freedom to change their religion, if they so wish.

Moral concepts such as "the inalienable right" of every man and woman "to life, liberty and the pursuit of happiness" stem from the belief that every human being deserves to be treated justly and fairly before the law but, at the same time, if we allow people unimpeded free rein to exercise their worst impulses, then we will all suffer.

Atheists, however, have mockingly said that those high-blown principles, worthy as they are, have proved not to have been sufficient to effect the immediate abolition of slavery in the USA. In fact, several signatories to the American Declaration of Independence owned cotton plantations manned by slaves. As a result, the country was convulsed in a Civil War 160 years ago. The other evil, prejudice and racial segregation, persisted for many more years until it was finally abolished by law after the Second World War. Furthermore, say the atheists, the biblical injunction "love your neighbour as yourself" has been proved to have been totally ignored as regards the conduct of inter-national affairs. There have been two horrendous World Wars and a plethora of minor ones during the course of the twentieth century. Some severe conflicts have, sadly, persisted right up to the present day.

One thousand years ago the Christian Church, which was originally founded on high moral principles of love, tolerance and compassion, seemed to have lost its moral compass as it embarked on a series of inhuman acts which resulted in the death of hundreds of thousands of people over several centuries. In 1096 Pope Urban II launched the first of several Crusades with the object of recapturing the holy city of Jerusalem. He provided religious justification for a "Holy War" against Islam, the then custodians of the Holy Land, and he was not troubled by the fact that thousands of Muslims and Jews died in the process. The Pope talked of "maintaining the peace of God". In fact, the mass killing of innocent non-combatants, and the immoral, unprin-cipled behaviour of the knights and their rabble of thousands of followers took place to the accompaniment of cries of *"Deus Vult!"* (God wills it!).

In 1252 Pope Innocent IV, seeking to demonstrate his power, authorised the use of torture to put down heresy. Two hundred years later the Catholic Church introduced severe laws which targeted anybody who did not comply with its beliefs. In Spain, Portugal and elsewhere a Grand Inquisitor was charged with the duty of harassing and pursuing anybody who was not a Catholic and attempts were made at forcing them to give up their previous religion, be it Judaism or Islam. Thousands of Jews were "encouraged" to abandon their faith and embrace Catholicism. Those who equivocated were condemned to one of two alternatives: either the sentence of death by being thrown onto the bonfires which were lit in public squares, or the forced expulsion from the country.

The Church even introduced the contemptible idea of "*limpieza de sangre*" (cleanliness of blood) in order to distinguish between real Catholics and those more recent converts, who were referred to as *Conversos* or, more contemptuously, as *Marranos* (little pigs or swine). The Jewish people have been, for nearly 1,000 years, at the mercy of fanatical Muslim mullahs and Christian priests who appeared to have cast aside the moral teachings inherent in their respective religions. In Muslim lands the Jews were classified as *Dhimmis* and they were subject to a special per capita tax, known as *Jizya*, and to various humiliating laws, such as restrictions on the sizes of their homes, the wearing of degrading clothes and the fact that, in any dispute with a Muslim, the Courts preferred to accept the testimony of a non-Jewish witness. Jews in Yemen were forced to clean the public latrines and to remove the carcasses of animals that were found on the roads.

Catholics have, over many centuries, put on "Passion Plays" during Easter, which were accompanied by vicious attacks on Jews and the burning of synagogues. Jews were forced to wear distinctive clothing and to live in certain designated cramped ghettos, usually located in unhealthy locations such as tanneries or iron foundries, in order to emphasise their inferior status. From time to time Jews were obliged to listen to Christian sermons and to take part in staged public disputations testifying to the "superior truth" of the Christian faith.

Thousands of Jews did, of course, abandon their religion and many converted against their will, under the deluded notion that they would be immediately accepted into society at large. Many more would not budge from their faith and they had to abandon their homes hastily in order to find a safe haven in a more tolerant country. The persecution of Jews by the Church and the attempts to convert them were made mainly on the pretext that the "unbelievers" needed to be forced to "see the light". Of course, there were other reasons, such as the baseless accusation that Jews were "Christ-killers", and there was some resentment at the Jews' economic success. The powers of the Inquisition continued officially until 1834.

Thankfully, we are now living in more enlightened times. Senior Catholic clergy, including the Pope, have in the past 60 years, shown contrition over the unjust treatment of the Jews and Muslims in former times. More recently, sincere regret and shame have also been expressed over the systematic abuse of young people by various members of the clergy of all religions, a scandal which has apparently been allowed to go unpunished over many decades.

In 2001 the world press reported that two monumental sandstone statues of the Buddha, which had been carved 1,500 years ago on the side of a hill in Afghanistan's Bamiyan region, were severely damaged by explosions of dynamite on the instructions of the Taliban.

Equally barbaric were the actions of jihadists associated with the so-called Islamic State, who have established a major foothold in Iraq and Syria, and who, in February 2015, have systematically used sledgehammers to destroy the monuments in the ancient Assyrian city of Nimrud. Not only were 3,000-year-old historical treasures ruined, the senseless thugs have apparently destroyed the tomb of the prophet Jonah in Nineveh and have even burnt several thousand historical books and priceless manuscripts stored in the Mosul Library. Similar mindless destruction has taken place in Palmyra, where Roman arches and other monuments dating back 2000 years have been blown up.

These deliberate immoral acts, the desecration of ancient religious and anthropological treasures, on the grounds that they were "non-Islamic," demonstrate extreme intolerance and they have been rightly condemned by UNESCO and all over the civilised world.

People all over the world equally were horrified when they learnt that several hundred schoolgirls in Chibok, Northern Nigeria, were forcibly taken away and their school premises were burnt down by armed men belonging to *Boko Haram*, an extreme Muslim sect which prides itself on the deliberate removal of all forms of "Western" influence. In December 2014 the Pakistan Taliban militants in Peshawar were responsible for the death of about 150 innocent people, mainly schoolboys and teachers, by detonating a satchel full of explosives in an army public school.

Actions such as those described above, which are immoral and unacceptable, sully the reputation of all religions; it cannot now be claimed that religious believers have a monopoly of compassionate behaviour, nor can the actions depicted above be paraded as examples of honourable or tolerant religious practice.

The Evolution of Moral Values

Standards of morality can and do change during the course of time and, as we have seen above, they are not common to all cultures and religions. A "universal moral law", which is what we are talking about here, does not exist in any written form, because many values emerge naturally, and they tend to undergo subtle changes over time. But we can apply a useful personal test: if I have been at the receiving end of a harmful action, deliberately perpetrated by another, or if somebody had used a form of words about me or my family in a derogatory or injurious way, how would I feel? There is no room for moral relativism here. If I find that the action or the words are distasteful or unfair or harmful then I must desist from taking a similar action or utter the same words against another person.

In the Bible, which was transmitted to the world through Moses, there are several references to conduct which would be unacceptable by today's moral standards. One obvious example is the attitude towards bigamous marriage, a practice which has persisted from time immemorial and which is mentioned several times in the Bible. In countries where eastern or oriental traditions were prevalent, men could quite legitimately be contractually married to more than one wife at the same time, but this practice has long since been deemed morally unacceptable and it is now abolished (at least in the "Western" world).

Elsewhere, the Torah records that when Moses came down from Mount Sinai, bringing with him the two tablets of the law, he saw that his brother Aaron had not taken appropriate action to forbid the construction of a golden calf for the purpose of worship. This serious lapse into paganism so enraged Moses that about 3,000 Israelites were put to death for this transgression. From today's vantage point this punishment appears to have been wholly disproportionate and excessive.

Again, we are informed that Moses and Joshua, who were leading the Israelites on the long journey from Egypt to the Promised Land, agreed that they had to wage war against the resident Canaanites before settling on the land of their vanquished adversaries. Apparently, there were special reasons for the sanctioning of such unprovoked aggressive behaviour on the part of the Israelites: the Canaanites were accused of practicing a crude form of paganism, including infanticide.

The permission which the Torah gives for the stoning to death of certain people who deviate from the biblical injunctions, such as homosexuals, is another matter which would not be acceptable behaviour in today's climate of opinion. Some atheists are contemptuous of the biblical injunction "an eye for an eye and a tooth for a tooth," but, of course, those who, quite rightly, scoff at such an obviously inhuman action have misunderstood the situation – it was only ever intended that monetary compensation should be awarded to the aggrieved person.

We are told, in any case, that these harsh laws incorporated in the Torah were hardly ever carried out in practice, and they were inserted as a red warning light, a signal that people ought to desist from unacceptable behaviour. It is also certain that, while these instructions may have been necessary in the primitive and agrarian communities of the past, these would today be considered totally redundant and unjust.

Set against those harsh and extreme edicts, however, there are far more wholesome Prophetic pronouncements, which are more in keeping with modern religious belief and aspirations, such as the following (from Isaiah):

"Nation shall not lift up sword against nation, neither shall they learn war anymore."

It is obvious that the commandment "Thou shalt not kill" is a moral principle which all fair-minded people today will wholeheartedly accept without hesitation. But that was not universally accepted six hundred years ago. As I describe in chapter 5, above, Aztec priests in Mexico believed that the deliberate ritual killing of hundreds of perfectly healthy, innocent, young men and women every year was necessary in order to propitiate the gods, ensure life-giving rain and thus avert mass starvation.

It is also worth noting that people's conception of good moral behaviour can undergo a complete revision even in a short period of just three or four generations. One hundred years ago, when several hundred British young men became Conscientious Objectors or Pacifists and refused to fight during the First World War, the overwhelming majority of the British population believed that this behaviour was immoral and deserving of utter contempt. The young men who refused the call-up were branded as cowards, women pinned white feathers on the cowardly men's lapels and some of the men were jailed.

Today, however, there appears to have been a complete *volte face*. In some communities memorial services have been held for the "conshees" who, some say, had been harshly treated in the past. The people who were mocked and abused one hundred years ago are now rehabilitated and they are considered to have been honourable men who, in compliance with their pacifist beliefs and conscience, were not prepared to carry a weapon and take another person's life under any circumstances. In 1995 the United Nations Commission on Human Rights specifically recognised the rights of people to express their strong moral objections to the pursuit of war.

Public acceptance of the need to atone for the unjust treatment of conscientious objectors is not the only example of a perceptible change in moral values. Some very prominent people, including a former Lord Chancellor, Lord Falconer, as well as a former Archbishop of Canterbury, Lord Carey, and Ian McEwan, the award-winning novelist, have all been campaigning in favour of the unprecedented legal right of people, who are in extreme pain and terminally ill, to choose when and how to end their own lives, provided there has been no coercion. The late Sir Terry Pratchett, the novelist, had campaigned in favour of assisted dying before he died of Alzheimer's in March 2015. Recently, several members of the House of Lords have added their voices in support of the relevant Bill which is currently being debated in Parliament.

Of course, all major religious figures in the world are strictly opposed to any form of euthanasia and assisted suicide on the moral grounds that it would be tantamount to "playing God." But some very sick people, who had been given a dire medical prognosis, have gone to great lengths to circumvent the present laws. Some have gone to Switzerland or Holland, where assisted suicide is allowed, and where special clinics have been set up.

The Times newspaper reported on 20th May 2014 that nine British Supreme Court judges were deeply divided over the extremely contentious issue of whether to allow doctors to assist those who wish to end their lives prematurely. But there is every indication that society, under the pressure of public opinion, will, within the next decade, tolerate assisted suicide under certain conditions.

Another example of the gradual and persistent tectonic shifts in standards of morality is the legal attitude towards homosexuality. Alan Turing was a brilliant mathematician and cryptanalyst, who performed crucially important work on deciphering the German Enigma machine during the Second World War. In 1952 he was found guilty of homosexual behaviour, which was deemed a criminal offence at the time. He chose to submit himself to chemical castration as an alternative to a prison sentence but, tragically, he committed suicide two years later.

British laws, which had criminalised homosexual behaviour for hundreds of years, have now been completely annulled and in 2013 Turing was indeed granted a royal pardon. Furthermore, in a complete reversal of the previous total antipathy towards homosexuals, a new law, passed in 2014, completely legitimises same-sex marriage. It is quite obvious that, on such matters as personal behaviour and life-style choices, a secular society does not wish to listen to the voice of the Church.

The Situation in Britain

On 15th June 1215 King John of England and a coterie of nobles met at Runnymede, near Windsor on the River Thames, in order to sign an important document, the Magna Carta. So began the long process which ultimately laid the foundation for constitutional law in Britain and the establishment of the House of Commons. Although Britain does not have a written constitution, Magna Carta provided the essential ideas, such as democracy and the rule of law, which have been crucial in shaping the governance of our country for the last 800 years. In recent months there have been several references to "British values" in the media, having regard to the apparent rejection of the commonly accepted concept of the "British way of life" on the part of certain immigrant communities.

In recent years the British government have been concerned over reports that the teachers or governors of some schools are deliberately propagating extremist religious ethics. It is feared that the pupils could be imbibing moral principles and codes of behaviour which are antithetical to the British way of life. Apparently, many schools in the Birmingham area are run on Moslem fundamentalist lines, where girls are made to sit at the back of the classroom and where science teaching is carefully monitored to remove any "controversial" topics.

Mr. David Cameron, the then British Prime Minister, referring to the extremist views being propagated in some schools, had to intervene to remind people that there are certain rules of behaviour and moral values which are inseparable from the British way of life and must be upheld. Just as we have a workable system of law and government which functions adequately without a written constitution, so we must adhere to a commonly accepted set of values and moral standards, even though they have not been formally committed to writing. Anything else would lead to a fundamental change in the nature of British society, leading to the abrogation of cherished beliefs such as the maintenance of the rule of law, the protection of minorities, the right to free speech and freedom of religion.

CHAPTER 9

Free Will and the Problem of Evil

"... We know beyond doubt that a human being's activities are in his own hands. ... The Almighty ... does not decree that (man) should act thus and not act thus. It is not religious tradition alone by which this is known. It is also supported by clear proofs furnished by science."

Moses Maimonides, "Mishneh Torah"

One of the fundamental Jewish beliefs, and one that finds a strong resonance in many other faiths, is that the Almighty has endowed mankind with the unique faculty of Free Will, the ability to distinguish and choose freely between different beliefs, lifestyles and courses of action. This attribute, to which Maimonides alludes, is unique to humans and it distinguishes us from other animals and, indeed, all other primates. It was first demonstrated in the Biblical story of Adam and Eve, which is presented to us in the form of a parable. The relevant verses of Genesis are imparting an important lesson, which can be stated as follows: throughout our lives on earth men and women will be confronted with situations and dilemmas, requiring a choice to be made between two or more alternatives. When we make a choice, when we decide on which course of action to take, we are doing so of our own free will. Assuming there are no undue threats or pressures from outside sources, we are each individually responsible for the consequences of our own actions.

The serpent, which is the embodiment of all our evil inclinations, uses its powers of seduction to tempt Eve into eating the fruit from the tree of knowledge. Eve succumbs to her evil inclination (*YETSER HA-RA'A* in Hebrew) and she takes the first bite. She then offers it to Adam, who also eats the fruit, even though he is aware that he would be committing a grave transgression. The couple chose to exercise their free will, they were in breach of a strict instruction, and they were eventually punished by being banned from the Garden of Eden.

Over the centuries some philosophers have been indulging themselves in an arcane debate, which can almost be compared to the argument over how many angels can fit on the head of a pin. If God is omnipotent, some say, and if He can predict all our actions in advance, can we truly say that we have been endowed with the faculty of unfettered free will? Is it not the case that, even before Eve succumbed to temptation, God must have been absolutely aware of the eventual outcome? That being so, how can we say that our putative ancestors had an absolutely free choice, untrammelled by any hint of Divine suggestion or interference, however indirectly?

Desiderius Erasmus, the famous Rotterdam theologian who lived about 500 years ago, during the time of the Renaissance, believed passionately that God created man with the important and unique attribute of free will. Ever since the days of the earliest *Homo sapiens* we have been endowed with the intellectual capacity to make conscious and deliberate decisions. In this matter Erasmus was diametrically opposed by his contemporary, Martin Luther, who propounded the alternative theory of "Determinism," a concept which came to be espoused by many Catholic reformers of the time. In the course of their heated debate and profound disagreement, Luther wrote to Erasmus, "free will does not exist."

The principle of determinism, which is the negation of free will, has a long history. Sir Isaac Newton, a deeply religious man, having discovered various physical laws of nature, believed strongly that there is an unbroken chain of events and prior occurrences stretching back to the first days of creation. Therefore, said Newton, free will does not exist. Supporters of determinism believe that all events have a pre-existing cause and there is no possibility for the element of chance to intervene. This was the view of the philosopher Thomas Hobbes and others, who pointed out that the Universe has always operated faultlessly, within fixed laws and with predictable accuracy. In his book, *"The Leviathan"*, Hobbes (who, some believe, was really an atheist) argued that everything about humanity can be explained materialistically, without recourse to an incorporeal, unseen Creator. If determinism was true, and if all actions are predictable by the Almighty, said Hobbes, then mankind cannot be said to possess free will. Incidentally, it was Hobbes who bequeathed to us a memorable turn of phrase. Having set out the arguments in favour of the maintenance of a strong central government or a monarchy, he said that, in pursuit of that goal, it was necessary for the citizenry to give up a small portion of their independence and free will. If people are not prepared to submit to the will of those in power, said Hobbes, mankind will rapidly sink to a "state of nature, and human life will deteriorate progressively until, ultimately, man's condition will become solitary, poor, nasty, brutish and short."

It is obvious that the main problem with accepting the principle of determinism is this: how are we to assign responsibility for any human actions, whether harmful or not, if they are deemed to be the direct inevitable consequences of the existence of past events?

During the nineteenth century events were dominated by the rise of materialism and the gradual decline of the power of faith. Charles Darwin's espousal of the principle of Natural Selection was part of the anti-religious feelings engendered by technological prowess, the rise in prosperity and the new scientific discoveries. Darwin attacked the biblical account of creation and he rejected the belief that man was created "in the image of God." He led the group of scientists who believed that mankind and all of nature were created naturally, by the natural laws of science, and not by Divine decree. The process of evolution, which he championed, was a corollary to his conviction that men and women have always had absolute control of our own lives and future, that we have rightly shaken off any residual allegiance to the Almighty and, as a consequence, Darwin believed that mankind does possess the attribute of free will and that we do, indeed, have the freedom and the capacity to take any action we wished.

Religious belief is in direct contradiction to that of Darwin insofar as the creation of the Universe is concerned. However, there is total agreement as regards free will, possession of which is certainly one of the cornerstones of Jewish and Christian faith. Men and women have been given the untrammelled capacity to choose their own individual moral goals and they can decide on the direction of travel in order to reach those goals. There are, inevitably, moral dilemmas when you are confronted by the need to make a choice between several alternatives. We need free will to enable us to weigh up the alternative courses of action and to make a choice that suits us best.

Men and women are not mere biochemical puppets on a string, the innocent prisoners of our genes, as atheists would have us believe. By and large, we steer a deliberate and wilful course through life from day to day. We are, in the main, autonomous persons; in the absence of any neurological disorder we can be considered to bear sole responsibility for our own actions. Most people will agree that they are not constantly subject to unreasonable pressure to commit a wrongful deed. Any other contention would undermine our concept of retributive justice.

Of course there are two kinds of freedom, one positive and the other negative. The first says that mankind has the absolute right and ability to take any position and follow whatever action we are minded to take, i.e. that we are masters of our own lives. Negative freedom implies that, in the exercise of our conscious desires and will, there must be a complete absence of undue interference.

We believe that free will can happily coexist with the demands of an omnipotent Divinity. The Bible makes this very clear. In Deuteronomy, chapter 30, verse 10, we see a clear reference to the power of choice in the following statement attributed to the Almighty:

"I have set before you life and good and death and evil ... therefore, choose life that you may live, you and your seed."

Today, scientists and others are prepared to accept, both philosophically and spiritually, that the "Principle of Uncertainty" applies both in the natural world and in the conduct of mankind and that the freedom to choose is a precious attribute. In other words, not everything is set in stone, and the concept of free will is alive and well. Man has the creative ability and the paramount need to control physical events, and we know that our actions can have a profound impact on one another and on the environment. As indicated by Maimonides, the great medieval sage and Bible interpreter, man is an initiator of change, and he is encouraged to exercise his free will where he believes that his actions will lead to the betterment of conditions on earth, in order to rectify anything which is actually or potentially harmful or in need of repair. In essence, therefore, there is no conflict between the seemingly contradictory concepts found in the Bible: we believe that the religious constraints upon men and women of faith do not really conflict with the moral independence which is implied by the possession of free will.

As a corollary to the concept of free will it is important to stress that it applies not only to the conduct of our lives but also to the promotion and enforcement of religious belief itself. It would be wrong for men and women to be forced, in a coercive way, to believe in any one faith, and, of course, there is no obligation to have any religious faith at all. As I point out elsewhere in the book, "all is in the hands of heaven except the fear of heaven." It must be left to every single one of us to work out and adopt any set of beliefs we may choose; we must be able to decide how we conduct our own lives.

Although the vast majority of us conduct our lives without making deliberate attempts to harm others, there have been some recent events which demonstrate the depths of depravity of some people whose evil inclinations outweigh any reserves of human sympathy they may have. The Jewish view, as expressed by Rabbi Akiva nearly two thousand years ago, is that you cannot blame God in heaven for the evil intentions and the actions of men on planet Earth. Instead of harnessing and developing their YETSER HA-TOV (good conscience), people who do evil things are described as being imbued with YETSER HA-RA'A (bad inclination). As I point out in chapter 10, below, when discussing the Holocaust, you cannot blame the Almighty for the evil deeds of wicked men. God endowed mankind with the attribute of free will and He does not determine or control the choice of actions dictated and motivated by an individual's free will. That God permits evil is still something of a mystery, but it is an unavoidable consequence of the possession of free will.

Baruch Goldstein was an American-born physician, a graduate of both Yeshiva College as well as the Albert Einstein College of Medicine in New York. He lived in the Israeli settlement of Kiryat Arba, near Hebron. On 25th February 1994, wearing his army uniform and insignia of rank, Goldstein entered a Moslem prayer-room in the Cave of the Patriarchs. Without warning he opened fire on the worshippers, killing 29 Palestinians and wounding more than 100 others. Eventually, Goldstein was grappled to the ground and beaten to death by survivors of the massacre. Following the shooting there were riots and even more deaths involving both Palestinians and Israelis.

The then Israeli Prime Minister, Yitzhak Rabin, telephoned the Palestinian leader, Yasser Arafat, to express his deep regret and shame at Goldstein's evil action. There was revulsion throughout Israel, Goldstein being described as a loathsome and insane murderer. When, a few months later, Goldstein's supporters built a shrine in his honour it was taken down by the Israeli army. In an ironic twist of events, Yitzhak Rabin himself was gunned down on the fourth of November 1995 by a Jewish religious fanatic, Yigal Amir, a mentally deranged young man who disagreed with Rabin's policies.

In July 2011 the world was transfixed by the news that a well-armed gunman had killed 8 people in a government building in Oslo, Norway, and then went on to kill even more people enjoying a youth outing on a neighbouring island of Utoya. Anders Breivik, aged 35, killed a total of 77 people and injured more than 300 others, most of them teenagers, in a calm and impassive manner. He was described as a bitter and twisted individual, he had delusions of grandeur, but the court found that he was not insane.

An equally abhorrent example of unmitigated evil occurred more recently. Malala Yousafzai was a schoolgirl, the daughter of Sunni parents, born in Mangora, in the Swat District of Pakistan. At the age of 12 she rose to prominence following her persistent criticism of the activities of the Taliban, a renegade group of Muslim extremists who were attempting to control the area, and who, in pursuit of their extreme Islamic ideology, wanted to limit the education of girls. The Taliban were attempting to wrest power from the legitimate government and they have been trying to impose Sharia Law by means of terror tactics, including murder and intimidation. They killed some of their opponents and exhibited their headless bodies on scaffolds.

In October 2012 Malala boarded her school bus as usual. A gunman, who was lying in wait, aimed a rifle at her and fired three shots. One bullet hit the left side of her forehead and it lodged in her shoulder. As a result of her horrendous brain injuries Malala remained unconscious and in a critical condition for several days. Later, she was allowed to travel to Britain where doctors in Birmingham carried out specialised surgery and intense rehabilitation. The attempted assassination of a fifteen-year-old schoolgirl caused revulsion, both in Pakistan and worldwide. In spite of continued threats, directed against both Malala and her father, she now continues her campaign to ensure that the education system for girls and boys in Pakistan will be at the same level. Malala is now internationally renowned and she has been invited to speak at the United Nations headquarters in New York. In October 2014 she was one of two people who were deservedly awarded the Nobel Prize for peace.

Other atrocious cases that come to mind include the terrible incident in Toulouse, France, where a Rabbi and his children were gunned down in 2012 and another case in Mumbai some years ago, again resulting in a young Rabbi and his family being killed in cold blood. Who can forget the assault and siege by about 6 or 7 gunmen on the Westgate shopping centre in Nairobi, Kenya, in September 2013, tragically resulting in about 70 deaths and nearly 200 injuries?

I wonder whether anybody has found the appropriate words to condemn the ruthless killing, in January 2015, of 17 people in Paris, some working at the office of a satirical weekly and others going about their shopping in a Jewish supermarket. These events will forever be seared on the memory of all civilised people of all religions and cultures.

Without the slightest hesitation we can condemn all the above crimes against innocent civilians whose lives were needlessly snuffed out, all resulting from a desire to inflict the maximum amount of terror and all perpetrated by evil men whose minds were twisted by ideology or the desire to achieve instant martyrdom or self-glorification. There is no excuse for such actions, irrespective of the religious or political motivations of the perpetrators.

All around us, there are men and women forever tempted to perform evil acts. As I have stated elsewhere, Judaism is not a coercive religion and we are all allowed to believe or disbelieve, to do the right thing or to commit an evil act. If it were possible to abolish evil overnight it would imply the negation of free will. It would imply that everything in life was predetermined by God. As a consequence, mankind would have no say in the conduct of our everyday affairs and no influence over our destiny.

The outstanding scientist of the twentieth century had this to say on the subject of evil:

"Evil is just like darkness or cold. (It describes) ... the absence of God. Evil is the result of what happens when man does not have God's love present in his heart ... just as cold is the absence of heat and darkness is the absence of light ..."

Albert Einstein, physics Nobel Laureate

Gottfried Leibniz, the seventeenth century mathematician and philosopher, developed the idea of Theodicy. This theological construct attempts to vindicate God, and to find the answer to the following question: if God is all wise and all powerful, how did evil come into the world? The answer, says Leibniz, is that while, on the one hand, God is indeed unlimited in wisdom and power, it is an incontrovertible fact that we, men and women, are limited in our wisdom; our evil intentions predispose us to false beliefs and to make wrong decisions. What makes it worse is that today we have the technological tools and expertise to commit virtually limitless damage on a vast scale.

It goes without saying that God, who is described as being full of CHESED (loving-kindness), does not inflict pain and suffering on any aspect of His creation. However, He seems to permit these bad things to happen. Some people contend that our knowledge of the effect of evil may have an unexpected positive effect: it nudges the vast majority of us towards the opposite extreme, the establishment and promotion of a good conscience, in turn leading to good and kindly conduct. After all, there is no virtue without the freedom to sin. Could it be, therefore, that God allowed some evil to creep into His creation in order to act as a warning signal, as a demonstration to humanity what can happen when people are minded to stray from the right path and commit evil acts? If we have not seen evil with our eyes how do we know whether our action in a particular case is deemed to be good or bad?

There is a Kabbalistic thought, called *TZIMTZUM*, which implies that, in the early moments of creation, God withdrew Himself very slightly from the creative process in order to allow room for the development of the Universe. His partial and temporary withdrawal meant that the Universe that was created lacks the full exposure to God's all-perfect nature. If you refer to the Book of Isaiah, chapter 45, verse 7, you will see the following:

> *"I (Yahweh) form the light and create darkness. I make peace and create evil. I, the Lord, do all these things ..."*

It seems, therefore, that evil is an inevitable part of the optimum combination of elements that comprise the best possible Godly choice. Our free will, coupled with our ambitions and the strong urge to strive and succeed, seem to create conditions for the existence of evil. On the other hand, if the Almighty had not granted us free will, then mankind would have remained in a perpetually savage state, since nothing would have been lacking, and everything would have been easily available, within arm's reach of desire.

If evil did not exist, if we were not confronted by temptations all around us, there would be no need for us to possess the faculty of free will. In a utopian society, where evil is somehow expunged, there would be no need for mankind to decide, day after day, what is right and what is wrong.

CHAPTER 10

Pain and Suffering:
The Eternal Dilemma

"I don't like people who have never fallen or stumbled. Their virtue is lifeless and it isn't much of value. Life hasn't revealed its beauty to them."

Boris Pasternak, *"Doctor Zhivago"*

There is no denying that, in the course of our lives, most of us may, from time to time, experience severe pain, either physical or mental, or we may need to deal with a personal tragedy, the result of circumstances outside our control. It was ever thus. Most people stoically accept and try to cope with moments of sickness or tragedy experienced by them or by members of their extended family. Optimistically, we harbour the hope that the suffering will only be temporary and we may look forward to the future in the hope that the wheel of fortune may one day turn in our favour. But, equally, there will be large numbers of people who feel that they need to express rage at the unseen God and wonder why they have been singled out to be the recipients of an episode of great unhappiness or unbearable physical pain. They may even cry out: "Lord, what wrong have I committed? Why are you not listening to my prayer?"

The truth is that the existence of sorrow and pain does not automatically preclude the possibility of the existence of God, just as we cannot positively prove His existence merely by recalling moments of bliss and success in our lives. You cannot logically say that God is to be blamed for the fact that some people are experiencing trauma, suffering and loss.

The Biblical story of Job highlights the issue of a righteous man who suffered terribly and who was severely tested, almost to destruction. Satan, a demonic figure, believed that Job's apparent piety was superficial and, if placed under duress, Job could be made to abandon his belief in the Almighty. In quick succession Job loses his children and all his possessions, and yet, in spite of his terrible reverses, his devotion to God is unshaken. His response is limited to uttering words which have now formed part of Jewish liturgy: "The Lord has given and the Lord has taken away; blessed be the name of the Lord."

Job is then afflicted with disease, and his wife urges him to remonstrate with God. God's answer to Job is the one which most people of faith will understand: He reminds Job that His own ways are beyond the understanding of mortal man and will remain a mystery. Today, reading his story, we can empathise with Job's anguish, and, in relation to our own lives, we can offer words of sympathy and support to those of our family and acquaintances who are in need of help. But, as to the reason why so many of the guilty prosper or so many of the innocent suffer, that is not within our power to comprehend.

Is it possible to make a connection between Job's horrendous experiences, on the one hand, and the sufferings endured by

millions of innocent men, women and children during the Holocaust on the other? Of course there is a close parallel. I do not
believe that the agony of millions of people living under the heel
of the Nazis during the 1930's and 1940's was a form of retribu-
tion for any past misdeeds of the ordinary people, both Jewish
and gentile, as has been alleged by some thoughtless people. And
it is grotesque to believe that there was an episode of *HESTER
PANIM*, i.e. the notion that God was, so to speak, "hiding His
face" from the Jewish people, for whatever reason. Modern
Jewish opinion rejects the view that there exists an active,
personal, finger-wagging God, constantly ready to administer
vengeful punishment in that direct way. On the contrary, our
belief is that the Almighty is full of loving-kindness who allows
us to reflect on our actions and repent if appropriate.

The vile concentration camps and the deadly gas that killed
so many were the products of the minds of evil men and women
who acted of their own free will and from the basest of vile
motives. The late Rabbi Hugo Gryn, who was born in Czecho-
slovakia and whose family suffered grievously in the holocaust,
has said that the blame for the suffering of millions of people
during the dark and tragic days of the Second World War must
rest squarely upon mankind itself.

The truth is that the evil men at the top of the Nazi hierarchy,
together with large sections of the people who came within their
ambit, had lost all sense of human compassion and they chose to
behave ruthlessly towards people who were perceived as "inferior". Under the influence of a warped belief in their own racial
superiority they discarded their moral compass and they used
their skewed theories to justify their murderous and horrendous
crimes against 12 million innocent civilian people, of whom 6
million were Jews. And these figures do not include the many
millions more who died in the fields of battle during the terrible conflict which the Nazis instigated. Humanity as a whole,
not God, must assume full responsibility for the perpetration of

those tragedies. With enough political will, courage and imagination on the part of the forces confronting the Nazis, maybe they could have found ways of blunting the Nazi leaders' evil intentions, with the result that millions of innocent lives could have been saved.

Apart from the various examples of unconscionably evil and barbaric behaviour perpetrated by people against their fellow men and women, and away from the arenas of conflict and warfare, there are, of course, uncounted examples of natural disasters and pestilential diseases which have blighted human history since time immemorial.

Huge numbers of people in the Eastern Mediterranean region were killed in the 6th century CE as the result of bubonic plague which originated in China, while the much more serious Black Death, 800 years later, killed about 75 million people, estimated to be 50% of Europe's population. Another tragic pandemic raged for 2 years in 1918-20 when more than 50 million people perished due to a deadly influenza virus, wrongly nicknamed "Spanish flu."

In December 2004 more than 250,000 people died and countless people lost their homes and livelihoods when a tsunami struck in the seas around Aceh (Indonesia). The devastation was felt in many areas including Tamil Nadu (India), Sri Lanka, and Thailand. The undersea earthquake, resulting from the collision of tectonic plates, registered more than 9 on the Richter scale and its ramifications spread far and wide.

More recently, in May 2008 an earthquake with a magnitude of 7.9 on the Richter scale struck the Sichuan region of China. It is estimated that some 70,000 people died and a further 370,000 people were injured on this occasion.

A devastating earthquake hit the Caribbean island of Haiti just a few years ago, virtually destroying the capital, Port-au-Prince.

Approximately 250,000 people died and thousands more were left either orphans or homeless.

Many people will recall that there were two major natural disasters in 2011, prompting a flurry of speculation concerning the nature of God and the limits of His powers. In February of that year a major earthquake struck the southern island of New Zealand, with the epicentre located about ten kilometres south-east of Christchurch. In all, the few seconds of terrible earth tremors, together with the frightening aftershocks, resulted in at least 185 deaths. Hundreds more were injured or suffered materially and the damage to thousands of buildings in the vicinity was quite severe. The cost to the New Zealand economy has been put at $40 billion and it is estimated that it will take at least 50 years for the country's economy to recover its losses.

In March 2011 a huge earthquake and tsunami struck Japan which, apart from the horrendous human casualties, also caused severe damage to three reactors at the Fukushima Daiichi nuclear power plant complex. It is thought that this was the biggest ever earthquake in Japanese history, resulting in nearly 18,000 deaths, 6,000 human injuries and it is feared that there are 2,000 people still classified as missing. The quake and the related aftershocks were felt in different parts of Japan, far from the epicentre, causing damage to thousands of buildings. The World Bank has estimated that the total cost to the Japanese economy as a result of this one event is in the region of US$235 billion.

During the last few days of April 2015 the world's media was rightly focused on the terrible consequences of the earthquake in the Himalayan state of Nepal. Residential buildings and Buddhist shrines across vast areas of the country, including the capital, Kathmandu, were turned into rubble and it is feared that 10,000 people died, including many mountaineers.

So we can see that, over the span of many centuries, natural disasters have exacted a heavy toll on humanity. According to one estimate more than 120 million people all over the world have died due to natural disasters in the last 100 years alone.

The mocking and unfeeling comments emanating from the atheists and humanists were entirely predictable. They had a field day because they could now utter their scornful jibes: "how can you have faith in a God who, having created the Universe, then retires from His labours, apparently very weary, or perhaps somewhat uninterested in our global welfare? Why does God not intervene to prevent natural calamities such as earthquakes, avalanches, tsunamis and pandemic diseases? Why does He do nothing about the deadly Ebola viral disease which has blighted the lives of three West African states for several years, and which has affected about 20,000 people of whom 11,000 have already died? Is He deaf to humanity's heartfelt pleas? Has religion nothing to say about the large number of deaths, the break-up of families and the massive destruction of livelihoods?"

Of course, nobody wishes to belittle the trauma and the sense of distress and pain caused to those who were caught up in the New Zealand and Japanese tragedies, as well as the agony of people caught up in similar tragedies resulting from geophysical forces, such as the earthquakes and typhoons in China, Haiti, the Philippines and Nepal, or the spread of disease elsewhere in the world. The suffering is real and palpable, our hearts go out in sympathy, and we are prompted to offer words of comfort and, where possible, physical and material aid to those involved.

What is the Theistic Response?

What is the response of religious people to the pain and suffering resulting from natural calamities? Men and women who believe in the Almighty should, by now, be aware that the various heavenly bodies coalesced and were shaped while incorporating various built-in constants and necessary features: the existence of unstable tectonic plates constantly migrating over the entire globe, the laws of gravity, electromagnetism, the background nuclear forces, the behaviour of liquids and gases when exposed to differences in temperature, the sudden variation in wind patterns, the effect of the moon on the tides, and the various changes in climate and rainfall due to the seasons. All these geological and natural features are part of the world's make-up; they are inescapable and, inevitably, they sometimes erupt in an adverse geophysical manner.

Our sages do not accept the notion that a perfect God would, naturally, have created a completely finished and ready-made world that is free from disease, free from human suffering, free from risk and natural calamities. We have to accept that there will always be periodic realignments of tectonic plates, volcanic eruptions, typhoons, earthquakes, floods, blizzards, landslides and severe drought in different parts of the world and all these natural phenomena will continue to occur inexorably and unpredictably. However, the Almighty calls upon us, all mankind, to help in the quest for the amelioration of our lives. We are God's partner in the process of creation and evolution and we have an everlasting and constant duty to help in repairing and reshaping the conditions around us so as to minimise risk and introduce more comfort into our lives.

Let me say something else about the intervention of the Almighty in our daily lives. Do we really want God to be unpredictable and interventionist, a God who capriciously intervenes in some disasters while abandoning others? We all know that there are certain laws of nature which apply impartially throughout the world. If I hold a coin in my hand, and I then let go of it, I can be sure that the law of gravity will cause the coin to fall to the ground. It would be bizarre if, instead, the coin flies up to the ceiling or if it floats away through the open window on my right. Similarly, it would be bizarre if, just for a few seconds, or for a day or two, supernatural forces are seen to cause the laws of nature to be thwarted, amended or suspended for the convenience of a certain selected group of endangered people. Our humanity, our freedom and capacity to act for ourselves would be destroyed if, just when a natural calamity (such as a blizzard or tsunami) is about to occur, the Almighty were to stretch out His hand, metaphorically speaking, and cause the winds to abate or the huge threatening waves to roll backwards, or if people were seen to be levitated away from danger in a magical sort of way. Do we expect that intervention to be on a selective basis? Do we want God to save, say, 10,000 people from the tsunami in Japan while, in another part of the world, He allows the death of 170 people in a New Zealand earthquake? Do we want Him to act in such a way that He will arbitrarily bring about joy and relief to some while others will be left to shed bitter tears of loss and sorrow?

We all have friends or relatives who have responded in different ways when dealing with their own sickness, pain and suffering as well as any trauma experienced by a relative or close friend. Some of us may know of friends who have been married for many years but who have remained childless, causing them extreme anguish. The different and very understandable reactions of people who are suffering severe trauma or setbacks of one sort or another can be summarised as follows:

This life is not all that there is. After death there is another world where we will find that all adversity is banished, life will then be sweet, free from strife and all our desires will be met. We must cope in this life as best as we can while we try to help others.

The philosophical approach is to believe that our suffering, although painful and unbearable at the time, allows us to grow in fortitude and acceptance, while our relatives and friends are presented with an opportunity to offer a kind word or an act of human kindness by way of moral support.

The defeatist or negative approach is to believe that life is full of pain and injustice. Some might say, "I cannot see why wicked people all around me are not being punished by God, and I cannot understand why my appeal for the alleviation of my suffering is not achieving any results. I am sure that God is not listening to me and I therefore see no need to believe in Him." A similar comment could have been made by people who have suffered a terrible bereavement, such as the death of a young child or a close relative of tender age through an incurable disease.

Of course, the last response, though understandable, can be rejected out of hand. I prefer the approach which says: God exists and, yes, suffering also exists. Now, let's assess the situation and be proactive in trying to eliminate the underlying cause of the pain and distress, if we can, so that other people will not suffer in a similar way.

This response to the dilemma of pain and suffering is both logical and practical. We all know that no sentient life exists without some pain, no life exists forever. Whether one is referring to a holy man with a prayer on his lips, constantly studying the scriptures, or an innocent little girl joyfully skipping with her friends in a school yard, tragedy can strike at any moment without warning. Life is fraught with risk, very few things are predictable. Let us consider the alternative. Would you really prefer a pattern of life which is completely ordered and predictable? How would you view the prospect of a world where pain and tragedy are somehow removed, never to return? Can you imagine a world of seven billion robotic individuals, all programmed to do God's work, all singing praises to the

Almighty and all constantly free from sorrow, ill-health or worry? Such a world, where all our needs are anticipated and fulfilled, where our date of death can be predicted with some accuracy, would be peopled by unfeeling automatons, where there is no need for anybody to come to the aid of anybody else, whether neighbour or stranger. In such a world, there would be a negation of suffering, an absence of tears. But it would also be a world where the precious faculty of free will is withdrawn, a world where there is no risk-taking and, consequently, no progress takes place.

God has endowed mankind with free will and the capacity to choose. Much of human progress stems from the fact that some of the more adventurous among us are able to imagine a better world and they may, of their own free will, choose a course of action which could potentially be very risky, but was designed to improve our life on earth. During the course of world history many individuals have undertaken perilous journeys of adventure or exploration; others have been called to the flag to fight for their country. Nobody can guess in advance which intrepid navigator will die in the course of their travels and nobody could have foretold which soldier will end up buried under a memorial stone in some foreign cemetery as a result of their endeavours in the defence of their homeland.

On the other hand, it is also true that many human tragedies are the result of the foolish risks we choose to take for ourselves. We choose to smoke that daily packet of cigarettes even though we are told that smoking has a deleterious effect on life expectancy. We choose to swallow the fourth double whisky before we get behind the wheel of our car, we choose to climb Mount Everest or indulge in skydiving, and we choose to go off-piste in order to get an extra thrill on the ski slopes. If, as a result of the risks we choose to take, we stumble or injure ourselves, we have no right to blame anybody but ourselves for our own misfortune.

Healing an Imperfect World

There is an important Jewish maxim which goes back to Mishnaic times and it is called *TIKKUN OLAM* (healing and repairing the world). Rabbi Joseph Soloveitchik, born in Belarus, who later became an outstanding modern American authority on Jewish ethics, said:

> *"When God created the world He provided an opportunity for ... man to participate in His creation."*

In other words, mortal man is encouraged to repair the flaws in the structure of the world and to make cautious adjustments to suit our convenience. The origin of the term *tikkun olam* is Mystical and Kabbalistic but it is, nevertheless, a powerful notion. Rabbi Akiva (he died in 135 CE) and other Talmudic Rabbis said that, whereas God is, of course, perfect, the world He has created is incomplete and imperfect. It looks as if God has empowered us to take part and complete the work of creation started by Him.

Tikkun olam says that God has given men and women the creative instinct, the capacity and the incentive to improve our earthly life. Each of our restorative acts brings a little piece of harmony to the cosmos. Each beneficial act mends a fracture of the world. Let me give you just a few examples of the concept in action.

You may recall that, many years ago, Dr. Jonas Falk and Dr. Albert Sabin succeeded in developing a vaccine to combat the scourge of polio which was endemic worldwide. Their medical endeavours were an outstanding contribution to the health of mankind and an excellent example of *tikkun olam*. Fifty years ago the number of polio cases worldwide amounted to many hundreds of thousands every year. In 2013 there were just 406 new cases and these occurred in Pakistan, Somalia and Nigeria, areas where the medical facilities are not of the highest calibre. In recent years polio has been spreading in Syria, a country whose medical services have collapsed due to an ongoing civil war, leading to a reduction in general immunisation.

Some years ago Bill Gates, the billionaire founder of Microsoft, created a medical foundation, one of its aims being a global attempt at finding a long-term cure for malaria, in the hope that this deadly mosquito-borne disease can be permanently eradicated. Huge efforts have been made in this direction; the wonderful and exemplary enterprise can be considered to represent an outstanding example of *tikkun olam.*

Medical teams from many nations have, quite rightly, rushed to the aid of victims of world-wide natural calamities such as earthquakes and tsunamis. It is heartening to see that Israeli doctors and nursing staff were among the first to set up medical and rescue facilities in Haiti, Japan and Nepal after their most recent terrible ordeals. In March 2014, as a result of the violent confrontation between Russia and Ukraine, several people died and many were injured. Some of the sick Ukrainians were offered on-the-spot humanitarian relief, while others were airlifted to Israel for specialised treatment.

I have read reports that during the past five years more than 4,000 injured Syrians, casualties of their internal political upheaval and civil war, have been given appropriate treatment by Israeli medical teams who have set up clinics on the border between the two countries, even though, in theory, Syria and Israel are still technically at war with each other. Israeli medical expertise has also been extended to several Palestinian leaders and their families even though there is a long-standing state of conflict between the two peoples.

Shimon Solomon, who was born in Ethiopia, now lives in Israel. He became a social worker and educator and he is the leading light behind the establishment of a unique children's village in Rwanda, in the heart of Africa, which is designed to nurture and care for the survivors of the genocide which occurred in that country about 20 years ago. That internecine eruption between the Hutus and Tutsis led to the tragic death of 800,000 people. Shimon Solomon's healing efforts are providing a shining example of *tikkun olam* in action.

We have all experienced a situation in our own lives that is akin to a miracle, a departure from the expected course of events, which has proved beneficial in the long term. I know that, in my own family, there have been 3 or 4 major sequences of events which have proved life-changing. I call them family miracles, gifts from the Almighty for which we are, privately, eternally grateful. However, the world is unlikely again to witness anything as spectacular as the parting of the Sea of Reeds. The age of great miracles seems to be over. This does not mean that mankind must lose hope and abandon the practice of prayer. Natural disasters will continue to occur. What we have to do is to cultivate qualities of forbearance and acceptance, and we must develop the important attribute of emotional resilience. Very importantly, we must use our reserves of compassion and brotherliness in order to extend a helping hand to those in distress.

CHAPTER 11

Ditching Religion

"If there are no guiding ideals to point the way, the scale of values disappears, and with it the meaning of our deeds and sufferings. This leaves only negation and despair. Religion is, therefore, the foundation of ethics, while ethics are the pre-supposition of life."

Werner Heisenberg, physics Nobel Laureate

Five thousand years ago our ancestors living in the Stonehenge area of England's Salisbury Plain decided to place some gigantic stones close to each other in a particular formation. At about the same time people living on the Isle of Lewis in the Outer Hebrides put up the Callanish Standing Stones and the same thing happened in Skara Brae in the Orkneys, as well as in many other parts of Ireland, Wales and Cornwall.

The question that has not been definitively answered to this day is this: why did these early Neolithic people, possibly clad in animal skins and wearing crude leather footwear, feel it necessary to exert their brute strength in order to haul these monolithic stones, some weighing up to 20 tons, across rugged terrain, and place them in a circular pattern? Were the rings of standing stones designed as a backdrop to some sort of ceremony, as a way of paying homage to the solstices, or were they perhaps to mark some elaborate religious burial location?

Meanwhile, thousands of miles away and almost contemporaneously with the boulder-displacement activity in Europe, workmen in Pharaonic Egypt were being directed to construct huge pyramid structures. Using primitive tools, they were able to quarry thousands of tons of limestone and granite. They shaped and meticulously aligned the huge stones, the whole construction demonstrating a high degree of precision and skill, all in pursuit of a quasi-religious objective related to some sort of burial ceremony.

Many years ago I had the opportunity to stand in the desert sands of Giza, within a few metres of the pyramids and not far from the Sphinx. One cannot help being hugely impressed at the fact that these structures still exist today, testament to the devotion, imagination and ingenuity of the ancient Egyptians. These massive monuments remain the very last of the seven wonders of the ancient world still standing. In fact, until the Eiffel Tower was built in Paris during the nineteenth century, the great pyramid was the tallest man-made structure in the world.

And it is not only in Europe and Egypt that we find vestiges of ancient spiritual activity. All over the world our ancestors have, over the centuries, bequeathed to us clues testifying to their need to express their latent religious yearnings. Ever since our ancestors started living in settled communities, some 9,000 years ago, people have considered it important to honour the memory of their ancestors, or make contact with the spirits, or commune with the unknown forces which they believed they had to worship or appease. Many centuries earlier our ancestors painted and etched on the walls of caves or carved crude fertility figures, again presumably for some quasi-religious purpose.

Today, however, many cynical philosophers, particularly those of an atheist persuasion, say that grown-up men and women do not need elaborate religious rituals. They say that we have grown out of the need for moral directions derived from religious texts, and the time has come to expunge all religious manifestations, because we do not need to be told how to behave in any given situation. They say that men and women are naturally endowed with a moral code which is ingrained from birth and, they say, to attempt to search for an objective or rationally justifiable code of ethics is to search for a chimera. I have recently come across the following comment in a book written by a leading atheist philosopher:

> *"... It must be possible to remain a committed atheist and nevertheless find religion sporadically useful, interesting and consoling ... It must be possible to balance a rejection of religious faith with a selective reverence for religious rituals and concepts."*
>
> Alain de Botton, "Religion for Atheists"

Alain de Botton grew up in an atheistic household. Although not wishing to be personally circumscribed by any formal religious belief and practice, he can still see the undoubted value of religion. It is refreshing to find a committed non-believer who is prepared to acknowledge the many advantages which are readily available to people of faith. He can see that, worldwide, all religious traditions have had an unrivalled record in promoting good deeds, establishing medical and educational facilities of the highest standard and inspiring outstanding music, architecture and art. He seems quite willing to cherry-pick some of religion's best features and he is valiantly trying to bolt them on, as an appendage, to a secular way of life. That will never work in practice. It would be equivalent to erecting a house, without foundations, on sandy soil. Such a society would not be able to withstand the brutal internal pressures of greed and self-interest which will soon develop if you knock out or weaken the religious foundations of society.

The whole tone of de Botton's book seems to hark back nostalgically to a worldview which he has personally scorned and rejected as worthless, but which, nevertheless, has found favour with millions of people over countless generations. He seems reluctant to let go entirely of "a host of consoling, subtle or just charming rituals for which we struggle to find equivalents in secular society." He comments favourably on the rituals of a Catholic Mass, which "strengthens congregants' bonds of affection" and, furthermore, he thinks that:

"The Jewish Day of Atonement is one of the most psychologically effective mechanisms ever devised for the resolution of social conflict. ... So cathartic is the Day of Atonement, it seems a pity that there should be only one of them a year. A secular world could without fear of excess adopt its own version to mark the start of every quarter."

All Alain de Botton is really doing is seeking to scrap one set of solid and long-standing beliefs and rituals (religion) and replace them with a set of ersatz beliefs (secularism) based on untried and untested theories. He remains in the vanguard of a movement which seeks to restore to secularists that which religious adherents have always taken for granted, namely, a life lived as virtuously as possible, taking guidance from a coherent set of religious principles and codes of conduct which have been tested over time.

He refers longingly to the time, years ago, when people were able to cope with "terrifying degrees of pain" by relying on the comfort of religious belief. There is no doubt that a certain degree of spiritual serenity can be achieved by reading selected passages of classical literature or by recalling a piece of well-loved music or reciting an uplifting poem. Alain de Botton acknowledges that a life lived in a spiritual way seems better able to cope with adversity, and he readily admits that modern atheism is less capable than religion at dealing with the many problems which we encounter every day. I cannot disagree with him when he writes that religions are:

"... repositories of myriad ingenious concepts to assuage ... the most persistent and unattended ills of a secular life."

One can disagree with much of de Botton's conclusions, one can reject all his atheistic panaceas, but nobody can fault him for the courteous manner in which he presents his views. His approach represents a marked contrast to that of Professor Richard Dawkins, the author of several best-selling books, such as *"The Selfish Gene"*, *"The God Delusion"* and *"The Blind Watchmaker."* Dawkins seems to enjoy being as confrontational as possible when he discusses the basis of religious belief. In pursuit of his evangelical atheism he has said that the Universe has no design, no purpose, no evil, and no good, nothing but blind pitiless indifference. He maintains that nature's building blocks, the cells, genes, etc., neither know nor care how or why they develop and multiply. Even so, in propounding the idea that all genes act in an undirected and selfish manner, Professor Dawkins made the following revealing comment in his book, *"The Selfish Gene"*:

" A human society based simply on the gene's law of ruthless self-ishness would be a very nasty society in which to live ... If you wish, as I do, to build a society in which individuals cooperate generously and unselfishly towards a common good, you can expect little from biological nature. Let us try to teach generosity and altruism because we are born selfish."

Here is somebody who has been in the forefront of the anti-religious movement but, amidst all the vitriol which he spews over mankind's inherited religious precepts, he cannot help but acknowledge that there is more to humanity than our purely biological nature. He advocates the need to teach generosity and altruism – two stellar features which lie at the core of all religious teaching and practice.

Do you have to belong to a religious group in order to be good? Of course not. Goodness should be its own reward. People of faith believe that doing good for the sake of some postponed heavenly benefit would undermine the concept of altruism. In other words, altruism (innate spirituality) trumps biology (innate selfishness).

Unless we have a heart of stone, all of us will, without hesitation, respond to a distress call from somebody who is injured and lying bleeding on the side of the road, whatever our moral and religious background. Our heart misses a beat if we see a child in imminent danger. If we encounter a case of wanton cruelty we do not have to be religious to empathise and register a suitable protest. If we are sitting in a bus and an elderly lady comes on board, laden with shopping, most of us will naturally offer her our seat without the slightest expectation of future reciprocity. These acts are prompted by our inherited spiritual nature, a gift from the Almighty, irrespective of whether or not we belong to any religious group. A strong feeling of empathy, a desire to help a neighbour or friend who is in distress or who needs assistance, they are all evidence of the spiritual attribute which separates us from other animals.

The various forms of religion, which have developed comparatively recently in our evolutionary history, consist of sets of practices and beliefs which have flowed naturally from our innate spirituality. Does that mean that you are devoid of moral sense if you are an atheist or if you have absolutely no contact with the teaching of any faith group?

I will answer this question by introducing the philosophical concept which some commentators have called "the cut-flower syndrome."

If I take a stroll in my garden and decide to pluck one or two beautiful flowers to place in a vase indoors I know that they will retain their beauty and fragrance for three or four days. But my action will have deprived the blooms from the full growth potential which they had previously derived from the nutrients flowing from their root systems. The same thing will happen with life-enhancing concepts such as hope, charity, freedom, brotherhood, justice, pity, mercy, dignity and the other virtues which most of us take for granted today. These virtues could very well shrivel and become atrophied if they are cut off from their religious origins. Most nation states today have grown and thrived by subscribing to principles of morality and fraternity which have been developed over many centuries, many of which originated from religious principles. If we cut off religious faith, if we decide that our country will henceforth be run on entirely secular lines, if we excise all reference to a deity from our laws, morals and behaviour, we run the risk of ultimate chaos. I would argue, therefore, that religious values and disciplines help to channel and reinforce people's natural desire to act for the benefit of society as a whole.

Without religion society may appear to prosper for a while as though nothing has happened, but it won't be long before things will start to fray at the edges. This is because the underlying basis of law and order as well as the conduct of government will be deprived of valuable moral principles inherited from the major religions. Religious principles and ethics provide the continuous nourishing and life-giving nutrients which allow society to live and flourish. Whether we are aware of it or not, we are, every day, drawing upon a huge bank stuffed full with guiding principles of good ethical behaviour and standards which have been accumulating over several millennia.

If religion were totally abolished how would mankind behave and interact with one another, not only today or tomorrow but in a hundred years from now? Dr. Francis Collins, a prominent American scientist and a committed Christian, says in his book, *"The Language of God"*:

> *"The concept of right and wrong appears to be universal among all members of the human species (though its application may result in wildly different outcomes) ... (Unlike) the law of gravitation or relativity ... it is a law that, if we are honest with ourselves, is broken with astounding regularity."*

It appears, therefore, that mankind's innate spirituality (a faculty not necessarily related to any religious affiliation) will provide most of us with a strong impulse to sympathise with and assist other sentient beings, whether human or animal. The desire to rush to the aid of our fellow men and women is a praiseworthy virtue, derived from our innate spirituality, something which only humans possess naturally. It is also true that some animals, such as elephants, apes, dogs and dolphins, do display signs of concern or a sense of loss if one of their family groups is injured, but their understanding is instinctual, quite limited in scope and nowhere nearly as developed as that of humans.

In the course of his lectures, and in the books he has published, Professor Dawkins has described the principles enshrined in the various holy books, as "vicious, sado-masochistic, repellent and barking mad." But Dawkins's comments and those of his atheist cohorts are irrational and totally without substance. The atheists and humanists are refusing to acknowledge the huge benefits which men and women all over the world have derived from the evolution of religious principles. Sophisticated human attributes such as optimism, hope, justice, altruism, fairness, happiness, charity and many others go beyond our inherited spirituality and have been introduced, refined and carried out through the filter of religious thought.

Atheists believe that "having faith" means a refusal to ask questions, and, furthermore there is the assumption that religious adherents are stuck in a time-warp. Nothing could be further from the truth. Jews are constantly encouraged to question, to search for answers and to keep an open mind if there are no easy solutions.

There are any number of examples to prove that people who are practicing members of a faith group are more likely to possess the precious faculties of kindness and charity. Had it not been for mankind's ubiquitous interaction and familiarity with these life-enhancing virtues, which we have naturally and unconsciously inherited from our sages and holy books over thousands of years, it is a safe bet that societies would now be conducting themselves in a much more unprincipled and lawless manner, and we would all have been the poorer.

Religious congregations absorb altruism and mutual sympathy as if by osmosis. There is strong evidence that they are more likely to be involved in providing networks of support to those who are sick or those going through a personal or family crisis. Troubles are halved and joy is multiplied when they are shared with other people. Even Karl Marx, the arch-atheist, had to admit that *"religion is the heart of a heartless world and the soul of soulless conditions."*

To be fair, atheists will be eager to point out that religions have every reason to feel very ashamed over their record so far. They point an accusing finger at leaders of religious faiths for initiating wars, causing bloodshed, mayhem and unrest over many centuries. If the *raison d'être* of all religions is the avoidance of discord, how do we account for the fact that, over a period of 2,000 or more years, that objective has not been achieved? Like an uncontrollable pandemic or a noxious miasma, religious wars have caused countless dead and utter devastation initiated by people who, at one time or another, have arrogated to themselves the badge of ultimate wisdom and who believed that they were acting in the name of their "just" religious cause.

Atheists love to dwell, quite justifiably, on the terrors of the various religious wars: the Crusades, the Inquisition, the Thirty Years War and the many current conflicts initiated at the behest of the Jihadists. If we agree with Mathew Arnold, that *"religion is morality touched by emotion"*, the corollary is that the emotion must be channelled towards wholesome and productive ends. The parallel here is with fire, which can warm your cold hands or make a nourishing bowl of soup, but, if left untended, can burn down your home.

Suppose that all the religions throughout the world were to disappear tomorrow, in a flash, how will society behave? Will there be a moral policeman to walk the beat, ready to blow the whistle when things get out of hand? How would men and women interact with one another, not only today or tomorrow but in a hundred years from now? Do we have sufficient in-built principles of morality which would guide the conduct of all mankind?

There have actually been some examples from history to demonstrate what happens when people attempt to excise religion from their lives and are willing to submit to be governed by people who had jettisoned any form of religiously-based moral guidance. The people of France went through a terrible time towards the end of the 18th century when, after a bloody uprising, the Bastille was stormed and the new "Committee of Public Safety" made a serious attempt to de-Christianise the country in the wake of the so-called "Enlightenment" period. Religion was one of the main targets during the violence, which was the consequence of the radical and social upheavals which convulsed French society after 1780.

There was huge popular resentment at the privileges and powers enjoyed by the Catholic Church and the bloated clergy. Under the influence of Voltaire and, in particular, Maximillien Robespierre, a period known as the "Reign of Terror" was launched, in the belief that men and women could govern themselves without the previous trappings of religion and the law.

The enemies of the people were perceived to be the nobles and, in particular, the priests. All the norms of morality were overthrown when, on the flimsiest of pretexts, some 17,000 people, including King Louis XVI, Marie Antoinette and hundreds of priests, died on the guillotine. It is estimated that as many as 30,000 others died in prison. In fact, among the many harsh measures introduced by the new secular government was the suspension of a suspect's normal right to trial and the removal of legal assistance to the accused before the death sentences were hastily imposed.

In the absence of the established organs of state and the rule of law Robespierre assumed dictatorial powers and there was a systematic effort to remove all vestiges of religious observance, as part of the anti-clerical wish to remove religion from the French way of life. There was an attempt to impose a 10-day week (thus playing havoc with the institution of the Sabbath), laws were hastily passed to introduce civic festivals, in place of religious ones, and all former privileges of the clergy were removed. It did not take long for the realisation to sink in that the removal of religious morality from the conduct of government was, in fact, a big mistake and Napoleon took over the reins of government in 1801 in order to restore some stability.

There have been more recent examples to show what happens to nation-states which are run on secular lines, free from the constraints and disciplines of religious morality. During the twentieth century, in the years between the two World Wars, the Soviet Union was governed by people who, in the pursuit of a godless Communist doctrine, considered that the individual rights of citizens came second to the needs of the state. Millions of people perished in the process, victims of the harsh dictatorial regimes, firstly under Lenin and then under Stalin. Whole communities were uprooted, there was compulsory internal migration, and attempts at forced resettlement involving hundreds of thousands of people as well as the collectivisation of agriculture. The whole gigantic upheavals were decreed and controlled by the masters of various centrally-controlled "five-year plans."

In Ukraine, formerly the bread-basket of the Soviet Union, more than 7 million people perished due to a series of policy decisions which came to be known as "extermination by hunger." All the harsh measures were introduced in tandem with the deliberate quelling of religious voices.

It is estimated that the communist regime of the USSR, together with that of the equally ruthless and godless Chinese regimes of Mao Ze Dong, Pol Pot's Khmer Rouge in Cambodia, as well as that of the Kim dynasty of North Korea, were together responsible for the deaths of nearly 60 million people, some due to starvation, others as the result of forced labour. Many people from all walks of life were summarily executed at the merest whim of the leaders and without the benefit of due legal process.

People living in countries headed by dictatorial or thuggish regimes have demonstrated that latent human aspirations regarding freedom of thought and freedom of worship are not easily stifled or eradicated. People do not want their personal beliefs to spring from diktats handed down by fickle political leaders.

The good news is that during the past 30 or so years there has been a sea-change insofar as the prevalence of religion in former Communist countries is concerned. The Soviet Union has collapsed and the former monolithic empire has been replaced by the Russian Federation, while the other states, formerly part of the USSR, have thrown off their shackles and declared their national independence. The people of Russia, Ukraine, Poland, and Hungary, the new Czech and Slovakian Republics and the other nations formerly under the communist yoke have been returning to religious observance in great numbers, in spite of being bereft of spiritual sustenance for several decades.

Today, after more than seventy years during which religion was obliged to maintain a low profile, there has been some major refurbishment of churches, and even some synagogues and Jewish communities have been given a new lease of life.

Similarly, the Chinese people have been granted limited freedoms ever since the country achieved its present unsurpassed status as an industrial and commercial superpower. It appears that, in the last twenty years, there has been a surge in the number of Christian adherents in China, and a serious attempt is being made at carrying out repairs and maintenance of the Buddhist Temples and pagodas. Several Chinese entrepreneurs openly admit that they have drawn freely upon Christian religious teachings in order to run their businesses on more equitable and fair principles.

Chinese Christians are now said to have reached 60 million and their number is predicted to grow rapidly to well over 100 million; China has the potential of becoming the country with the largest Christian population in the world. It seems that, in recent years, Chinese business success has grown side-by-side with an increase in religious adherence, with the one helping to boost the other.

Since the end of the Second World War there has been a perceptible enhancement of Jewish religious identity and adherence worldwide. In Israel and in the USA there are major religious seminaries and universities offering high-level courses in religion and history. In Britain we have seen a perceptible trend over the past two or three decades: a shift in Jewish population centres resulting in the gradual shrinking in the size of many provincial communities and a compensating growth in those located in certain other areas of London, Manchester and Leeds. This migration seems to be inspired by a desire of people to ensure a good Jewish education for their children and a preference for living in an area where there is a warm and vibrant synagogue and community fellowship. There is a palpable desire among our recently married couples to support and enhance Jewish education for themselves and their children, as well as an attempt to observe and maintain the laws regarding kosher food.

In the world as a whole the picture is uneven. In Britain there has been a marked fall in attendance at regular Christian churches and a newspaper reported recently the comment of some parishioners who have blamed this on the fact that "families are too busy juggling shopping, children's activities and home improvements." The Archbishop of Canterbury has even wondered whether British society is entering a "post-Christian era." However, there has been a boom in Church attendance in Africa, Asia, South America and USA.

So it seems that, in most countries, recent economic success has resulted in the need for people to tap into their spiritual

THE STORY OF HUMANKIND

roots and seek to establish a community spirit through the practice of religion. Many countries are governed by leaders who could be unpredictable and may potentially be tempted to succumb to political expediency, whereas organised religion provides essential continuity from one generation to the next. Political systems are fragile; religions seem to be more enduring and able to overcome setbacks and survive.

CHAPTER 12

Reasons to Believe

"Humans have always wrestled with the Divine Idea ... it is virtually certain that religious belief is as old as our species and it is equally possible that uncertainty, doubt and scepticism about God have existed since prehistoric times."

Lord Robert Winston, *"The Story of God"*

At the dawn of history our ancestors were tempted to ascribe to a god or to unknown invisible spirits any phenomenon of nature which they could not readily understand. The sun itself was invested with spiritual properties and many civilisations were in awe of celestial events such as thunder, lightning and eclipses. Some people were drawn to believing that the appearance of comets was an evil omen and, following such an occurrence, they had to brace themselves against potential dangers to come. Various animals (crocodiles, scarab beetles, jaguars, cows, monkeys, elephants) were worshipped because of their perceived superhuman or life-nourishing powers. Today, while science has explained much of the behaviour of celestial bodies, our relationship with the Almighty and with the natural world is more nuanced and multi-faceted.

In spite of God's physical invisibility, it cannot be denied that the Divine idea and the manifestation of theistic belief, as expressed in religious and cultural conduct, have been the most powerful forces that have shaped human behaviour over the past four or five millennia.

Belief in a deity has helped to mould the moral framework and the legislative priorities of many governments; it has shaped the structure of political institutions and the long-term aims and actions of several nation states. Alliances between nations have been welded in the name of religion. The religious evangelists' need to "spread the word" helped to fuel the growth in world exploration and the expansion of colonial empires. Religion has inspired the most sublime examples of artistic, literary and philanthropic endeavour. However, on the flip side, it must be said that, in the name of religion, millions have marched into battle and have been willing to die in wars against those who professed different tribal interpretations of the Divine idea.

But, while there are millions of people throughout the world who have always been comfortable in their belief in a deity, there have been many who have found it difficult or impossible to place their trust in an entity or a concept whose existence and power cannot be tested in a scientific way. Even so, in an age that is replete with technology, the paradox is that while there are many who insist on rigorous examination and proof, there are many more who are prepared to accept without reservation the moral message of the various holy scriptures and the pronouncements of men and women in all walks of life who have spoken of a loving God, clothed in majesty and power, a superhuman Being who watches over all His creation.

It is true that people today are more questioning; we do not accept any factual proposition without attempting, where possible, to seek unassailable proof. However, you cannot prove the existence of a deity by setting up a laboratory experiment. The existence of God is not something that can be demonstrated logically or rigorously. Belief is a matter of individual conscience; it is a matter of the heart. We are all, to a greater or lesser extent, flawed and hesitant believers, riddled with doubt. But the action of regular prayer tends to blow away the fog of disbelief from our hearts.

I have a two-fold objective in this chapter. Firstly, I want to give vent to some ideas which are germane in my adopting and supporting a theistic worldview. Secondly, I want to highlight the ideas of some people who have, over the years, challenged or expressed reservations in regard to the scientific theories propounded in the earlier part of this book. However, I am impressed by the following quotation extracted from Blaise Pascal's "*Pensées*":

> "*If we submit everything to reason, our religion will have no mysteries and supernatural element. If we offend the principles of reason, our religion will be absurd and ridiculous.*"

For most unbelievers, science has uncovered so many of the mysteries of nature that they are inclined to cast aside any notion that a deity plays any part in their lives. However, to a person of faith everything in life is refracted through the prism of his or her religious knowledge and worldview.

Atheists attempt to ascribe creatorial powers to "science" or "nature" or "the law of gravity." However, they fail to explain the original or ultimate author of these physical laws. It is hardly convincing to pretend that nature or science or physics were created "out of nothing."

Pure science cannot begin to provide comprehensive answers to such things as experiences, feelings and fleeting sensations, beauty or ugliness, joy or sorrow. Science has nothing to say about moral behaviour or altruism. Science did not invent the laws of physics and nature – the scientists' job is to dig deep, ferreting out and exposing the wonder and symmetry of creation. Scientists then use trial and error experimentation to confirm their findings.

It has become obvious that the symmetry and regularity must originally have been derived from laws created and imposed by God. As a result many modern scientists have begun to move away from previous scepticism and unbelief.

Teleological Considerations

There is one particularly attractive argument which supports the existence of a deity; it is easy to understand and it goes by the fancy name of "teleological". It is derived from a Greek word meaning "end" or "purpose" and it implies that everything has been designed and put in place to achieve a particular feature or result. It describes the perfect functionality of nature, with fine-tuned features dovetailing one with another, all in ordered beauty. The more that our scientists uncover details of the structure and workings of the Universe, and, in particular our own planet and everything within it, the easier it is to hold on to the conviction that everything in nature is too complex and well-ordered to have been produced by chance in an undirected or haphazard way.

Believers are inclined to say: look at the vastness of space, look at the incredible sophistication of nature, look at the regularity of the seasons, look at the wonderfully effortless ability of birds in flight, look at the symbiotic relationship that exists between one species and another, look at the very existence of life-sustaining water and other resources and look at the huge variety of micro-systems within our own bodies, incorporating checks, balances and rhythms which help to keep us alive and well.

Consider just one of the many complex features of our human body: the bilateral symmetry of our limbs. Who or what ensured the development of distinctive left and right hands and feet, in such a way that they complement each other perfectly, enabling us to carry out a variety of complex, vital and detailed tasks?

Theists, of course, relate the fact of creation to the desire of a supernatural and omnipotent Power, whom we call God, who wishes to have a loving relationship with all mankind.

Atheists, on the other hand, trumpet their belief that the creation of the Universe occurred naturally, and that it took place solely in accordance with the laws of physics. They assert that to invoke God in the creative process is to introduce an irrelevant and misleading hypothesis. However, many scientists have demonstrated that the chance that the creation of the universe was a completely random or accidental occurrence is so small as to be almost equal to zero.

As stated in the earlier chapters of this book, our sun shines brightly, day after day, due to the thermonuclear action taking place therein. There is a constant release of energy and a steady conversion of hydrogen into helium during the process known as nuclear fusion. It is surely a comforting thought that our sun will continue to shine brightly for the next five billion years. Bearing all this in mind, it is very hard not to stand in awe and wonderment at such everlasting, beautiful and sophisticated features as the intricate forces of nature, the stability of the atom, and the fact that molecules are able to self-replicate. All this cannot be dismissed as having been created entirely accidentally or thoughtlessly. Here are the considered opinions of three highly talented and thoughtful men on the subject of God and creation:

Arno Penzias, Physics Nobel Laureate, has written:

"(The idea of Divine) creation is supported by all the data so far."

Professor Richard Feynman, Nobel laureate in the field of quantum electro-dynamics, has said:

"Why nature is mathematical (and consistent) is a mystery. The fact that there are rules at all is a kind of miracle."

Professor Antony Flew, one of the world's leading philosophers, has recently written a book, *"There Is A God"*, in which he discards his former atheist beliefs:

"The argument for Intelligent Design is enormously stronger than it was .... it now seems to me that the findings of more than 50 years of DNA research have provided materials for a new and enormously powerful argument to (support the idea of) design."

It is perhaps appropriate here to highlight the distinction between "Intelligent Design" and "Creationism." ID is a scientific research programme which holds that certain features of the Universe cannot be attributed to random natural selection, as described by Darwin. Rather, say ID adherents, there are certain features which tend to betray a creative intervention by a superhuman Force. ID does not claim that it can detect any specific supernatural input *ab initio* – it merely uses hypothesis, experiments and careful scientific observation before it arrives at an appropriate conclusion. In spite of this "mission statement," ID has not been successful in deflecting widespread criticism, emanating from the legal establishment in the USA, that the theory cannot uncouple itself from its creationist (i.e. religious) origins. Creationism, which is specifically derived from a religious (i.e. a biblical) text, uses empirical evidence and it attempts to see how science and the religious texts can be reconciled, using the Bible account as the unalterable template.

The Lucky Universe?

Stephen Hawking once made the following very prescient (and almost theistic) comment, even though there is absolutely no doubt about his atheistic credentials:

> *"Why does the Universe bother to exist? If you like, you can define God to be the answer to that question."*

Both science and the Bible are agreed that creation took place at a particular moment in history. Once we move away from the concept of parallel universes and the idea of continuous creation you have a choice as to who or what was the author of that unique creation event.

Nobody has been able to provide a reasoned explanation of why there is "something" rather than "nothing." Nobody has yet been able to explain unequivocally the real physical origins of Big Bang and how it is that the Universe conforms to precise laws and symmetries.

Professor Stephen Hawking is on record as saying that creation occurred, quite spontaneously, in accordance with the physical law of gravity. But he has also pointed out that, at the time of Big Bang, if gravity had been just a tiny bit weaker, no stars or galaxies (and, therefore, no planets) could have been created. On the other hand, had the force of gravity been just a fraction stronger, the whole Universe would have collapsed or imploded before life could have got established. Furthermore, had the strong nuclear force, which exists all around us, been slightly weaker than actually occurred, then only hydrogen would have been created. Conversely, had the nuclear force been very slightly stronger, the result would have been that all the hydrogen in the atmosphere would have been converted into helium, and none of the heavier elements (e.g. carbon) would have been created. Both scenarios would have been fatal for the sustenance of complex life on planet Earth. In essence, then, had it not been for the superhuman calibration and fine-tuning of all relevant forces, we would not have been here to tell the tale. In another section of Professor Hawking's book, "*A Brief History of Time,*" there is a noteworthy and oft-quoted passage:

> "*Why is the Universe the way we see it? The answer is then simple: if it had been different we would not be here! .... The remarkable fact is that the values of these (fundamental numbers) seem to have been very finely adjusted to make possible the development of life.*"

It is true that, in more recent times, Professor Hawking has veered away from a theistic worldview, but in his earlier work as a physicist and cosmologist, he did express the belief that, "*So long as the Universe had a beginning we could suppose that it had a Creator.*"

Lord Martin Rees, emeritus professor of astronomy at Cambridge, believes that the carbon-based life on planet Earth was not arrived at haphazardly, but that we exist in a world which was "*tailor-made for man.*"

The pronouncements of both Professor Hawking and Lord Martin Rees prompt a layman like myself to ask: Who or what was responsible for the initiation and maintenance of all the so-called "laws" which govern our Universe? Who or what devised the physical constants: the force of electro-magnetism, the law of gravity, the constant speed of light, the strong and weak nuclear forces, the precise and steady movement of planets around the sun or the tilt of the Earth's axis?

Complex life is sustainable only because of the marvellous cosmological features which, I submit, were originally devised by a superhuman Mind. It cannot have been due merely to a lucky coincidence that the fundamental physical constants all happen to fall within the narrow range thought to be compatible to life.

Our planet, in common with the other planets, hurtles at an unimaginable speed through space, describing vast elliptical orbits round our sun, while maintaining a constant safe distance. In the absence of a Creator God, all sorts of probabilities and conjectures would have to take the place of our present safe, reliable planetary structures.

There is a Greek word, *anthropos,* which refers to mankind. The anthropic principle is a logical truism, based on the obvious fact that complex life would not have been able to evolve and thrive in conditions which turned out to be any different from those which have actually existed on Earth over the past 4 billion years. Professor John Polkinghorne has said that *"anthropic fine tuning is too remarkable to be dismissed as just a happy accident."*

If left entirely to chance planet Earth could have followed the fate of Mars – a cold, lifeless planet. Earth could have been locked into an orbit that was either too far or too close in relation to the sun. Our planet has been dubbed "Goldilocks" because, for reasons which the scientists are unable to explain, our terrestrial atmosphere is just right. It is not too thin and it is of the right density to maintain the presence of liquid, solid and gaseous water – all vitally necessary for the creation and maintenance of the carbon-based complex life that exists on our planet.

Another happy celestial circumstance is the existence of planet Jupiter, which should perhaps be labelled "Earth's Great Protector." Billions of years ago, Jupiter shielded us from the showers of meteors which were occurring during the aeons immediately after Big Bang. Many cosmologists believe that life on our planet would have been impossible today without the concurrent existence of Jupiter. Earth has a large and heavy metallic core made up of iron and nickel and this has created the magnetic field that was necessary to establish the Van Allen Radiation Belt. This has protected planet Earth from the constant harmful radiation bombardment from the sun.

Earth's crust is, on average, only 4 kilometres thick and the huge tectonic plates have a propensity to be constantly on the move. Over billions of years this activity has led to the formation of new continents and important geographical features such as mountain ranges. The tectonic movements are important in maintaining life and generating the essential process of the recycling of materials and nutrients. Had it not been for the existence and constant migration of the several tectonic plates our whole planet would have been covered by water.

By contrast with planet Earth, Venus has a 30-kilometre crust, there does not appear to be evidence of any tectonic activity and it is apparently devoid of any conditions necessary for the existence of any sort of complex life.

The atmosphere existing here on planet Earth is ideal. There is a thin layer, extending to about 60 kilometres above the surface, made up of the right quantities of oxygen and nitrogen. Had planet Earth been much larger than it is, (e.g. like Jupiter) the atmosphere would have consisted of a super-abundance of hydrogen. On the other hand, had Earth been smaller (like planet Mercury) complex life would not have been possible. Here is a quotation from an article written in the National Geographic magazine, dated April 2015, by Dr. Francis Collins:

> *"It is a miracle that there's a Universe at all. It's a miracle that it has order, fine-tuning that allows the possibility of complexity and laws that follow precise mathematical formulas ... there must be a "Mind" behind all this ... it is a profound truth that lies outside of scientific explanation ..."*

We can say that, as the result of anthropic fine-tuning, "nature" has contrived to provide the precise conditions that have allowed primitive life to be created and to diversify to such an extent that we, *Homo sapiens*, have acquired the power to become the dominating influence in our world. Atheists would say that the creation of that initial life-giving spark was entirely due to chance and a happy coincidence: i.e. the right elements just happened to come together at the right time, with the temperature being just right for life to be created. Can we believe in that totally accidental scenario, a many trillions-to-one chance event? Or, alternatively, can we, more reasonably, detect the guiding hand of the Almighty?

Origin of Life

There are those who equate nature with God, and some people of a scientific predilection believe that, while studying nature, one could be led into strengthening one's belief in the one God. As Albert Einstein has said,

"The laws of nature manifest the existence of a spirit vastly superior to that of men, and one in the face of which we, with our modest powers, must feel humble."

The fact that nature obeys laws, leading to the very creation and persistence of natural, living organisms, demonstrates the existence of a supreme Intelligence whom we call God. All life arises from a "First Cause" and that first cause must be omnipresent, omnipotent, outside our known Universe and eternal. Even the original Big Bang required a first cause, something which science has failed to explain satisfactorily. It was Louis Pasteur who said that *"life only comes from life."* Abiogenesis, a Greek word which makes reference to the creation of life from non-living material, is a most strange phenomenon, not compatible with or understood by science.

Geologists point out that rocks dating back to 4 billion years ago were totally inert and showed absolutely no evidence of latent life. And yet, about 200 million years later, the first miraculous steps occurred in the creation of life as we know it. Evidence exists that, about 3.8 billion years ago, the first living cells which were capable of storing genetic information were created. Very importantly, those living organisms were also capable of self-replication, and thus able to pass on their genetic information to their offspring. Science is not able to give us the answer to the following question: who or what created the many vitally important elements, the nucleotides, the molecules, the chemicals, and the protein-creation process? And scientists are still no nearer to answering the even more important question: who breathed life into those inert compounds?

The natural fined-tuned universe that we see around us must have originally sprung from a superhuman Mind. This is a fact that is evidenced not only by religious faith but also by the observance of natural reason. In recent years the strength of the so-called "argument-for-the-existence-of-God-from-observ-ing-design" has grown in strength and relevance.

Cells, Molecules, Genes, etc

Biologists tell us that every human body is made up of about 40 to 50 trillion cells, every single one a fully-automated factory directing and monitoring our development and growth. Each cell has an energy-producing system, a protective housing, a security system to let molecules in and out of the housing, a reproductive system and a central control system.

All living cells require nucleic acid (DNA) for replication as well as proteins to carry out the many activities needed to maintain the cell and support life. One cannot be produced without the other – a classic chicken-and-egg situation. There are hundreds of different types of protein and together they make up about 75% of the weight of a typical cell. In order to make a protein you need amino acids to link together in a chain. This linkage must occur in a specialised way and in a particular sequence, in the same way that the letters of the alphabet must be sequenced in a particular way to form an intelligible sentence. This requirement, called specificity, must be present before ideal structures are built within the cell.

A gene primarily consists of a genetic code, a language of systems and communications which provides a recipe for manufacturing proteins. The genetic message in DNA gets duplicated and copied through the availability of amino acids. This process occurs in an environment of microscopic mindless molecules. Proteins are made by the continuous process of sifting through and interpreting the message of the genetic code.

There is a huge range of what we call living organisms. For example, single-celled bacteria can make do with just 500 genes whereas every man and woman, while sharing the same genetic script as any other living organism, needs a total of about 35,000 genes in order to function. Even the smallest single-celled creatures are made up of millions of atoms forming millions of molecules that must be arranged in an exact pattern to provide the required bodily functions.

The "miracle" is that there exists a genetic mechanism that is constantly being created, within every living creature, which can transmit, from one generation to the next, information which has been sorted and which is capable of replicating – no mean feat! Nobody has been able to explain how this ingenious information processing machinery came to exist in the first place.

The question must be asked again and again: what is the likelihood that all this marvellous complexity, as described above, could have arisen entirely by chance, as the atheists would have us believe? Something or someone must have been present at the instant of creation and at the start of the evolutionary process that stretches all the way from the original microscopic one-celled living organisms that existed more than 3.5 billion years ago to the dynamic-seeking species that is mankind today.

Some years ago Professor Sir Fred Hoyle of Cambridge looked into the probability or practicability of producing even one single functioning protein resulting from a chance combination of several dozen amino acids. He came to the conclusion that the odds of this having happened by chance, billions of years ago, can be compared to the probability of a "roomful of blind men successfully solving Rubik's Cube simultaneously." He went on to ask witheringly: what is the likelihood that a completed Boeing 747 aircraft would be assembled if a massive whirlwind were to blow through a warehouse, full of aircraft spare parts, but with no organising or manufacturing intelligence to direct the whole production process?

And yet, as scientists have recently established, the most surprising feature is that more than 99% of every atom and molecule consists of absolutely nothing, i.e. completely empty space. With suitable high compression, the electrons in the bodies of all world humanity (all 7 billion of us) could be accommodated into a solid lump no bigger than a cube of sugar. Unbelievable but true.

Having described the function of cells and genes, let us consider just one organ of the body, the human brain. By any standards it is a marvel of construction and miniaturisation. It is only 1,350 cubic centimetres in volume, it comprises just 2% of our body weight and it works on minimum energy. We humans have over 86 billion neurons in our brain, and they are able to make instant communications with our other neurons, thus enabling the processing of one million messages a second. A neuron is a specialised cell that conducts electrical impulses. The signals between neurons occur via synapses (specialised connectors).

Our magnificent powerhouse of a brain can process, in one split second, information relating to the surrounding temperature, while simultaneously receiving and acting upon multiple messages related to colours, sound, mood, emotions and memories. And, all the time, it is controlling unobtrusively our breathing, eyelid movement, hunger, the presence of danger and many other bodily functions, such as the biological clocks and the circadian rhythms.

Scientists in Switzerland have recently started a project to build a huge replica of the human brain. It is being funded by the European Parliament at a potential cost of £900 million. Within the next 10 years dozens of scientists will attempt to put together a machine which will mimic the functionality of the human brain. They will need to install millions of miles of electrical wiring to do the work of our neurons. It is hoped that the machine will help in research, leading to the cure of neuro-logical diseases. Already, however, two daunting problems have become apparent.

The first is that the man-made brain, when completed, will need to be connected to a small dedicated power station, whereas the actual human brain runs very efficiently on as much energy as can be provided by one or two bananas. The second problem relates to miniaturisation – within a volume the size of a pinhead the actual human brain incorporates 3,000 potentially viable connections. It remains to be seen whether the man-made brain will ever be able to provide answers to some long-standing neurological and medical questions.

Of course, many scientists have been engaged in a never-ending quest to unlock the secrets of creation and evolution. But to get a measure of the huge task that lies before us, let us bear in mind that it took no less 20 years, an investment of a vast amount of money and the efforts of 10,000 scientists before the existence of the Higgs Boson could be confirmed! In other words, we have a formidably challenging task ahead of us.

Limitations of Darwin's Ideas

Many sceptical biologists are saying that we must be careful to distinguish between 2 types of evolution: micro-evolution and macro-evolution. Micro-evolution refers to the process described by Charles Darwin and consists of a very slow process, happening over several thousand or even tens of millions of years. Very few people dispute this. It is generally agreed that our pet dogs have evolved from wolves during the past 20,000 years and we know that commercial dog-breeders have consciously and deliberately emphasised or curtailed the characteristics of different breeds for commercial purposes.

This micro-evolution has been successful in removing undesirable biological traits over the course of thousands of generations. Unfortunately, it has also created some undesirable and unintended consequences as an inevitable by-product.

Macro-evolution, on the other hand, implies, for example, that the genes of a bacteria or a fish can evolve in such a radical and permanent way that, after several hundreds or thousands of generations, the progeny are able to discard, in successive stages, many if not most of the original features of that particular species. It implies that the original sea-creatures were able to leave their watery birth location and habitat, and, after many millions or even billions of years, they were able to evolve sufficiently so that they could transform themselves, eventually, into the human beings of today. This complete transformation from one species to another is what many people (including many biologists) find rather hard to accept because it is counter-intuitive and very hard to replicate under laboratory conditions.

It must be said that science has, so far, failed to prove how macro-evolution can occur and nobody has been able to demonstrate the mechanism by which new genetic information can be added to an existing species. Many people, including many scientists, find it hard to accept the possibility of "horizontal gene transfers," a theory propounded by neo-Darwinists. Every attempt at creating the laboratory conditions for a mutation to occur from one species to another (assuming it is allowable in law) has been crippling or self-reversing or even fatal. Yes, you can stitch a pig's trachea or bladder onto a human in order to replace an existing diseased organ, but you have to pump huge quantities of immuno-suppressant chemicals to fight against the inevitable rejection process. There are formidable in-built defensive mechanisms in our bodies that battle constantly against intruders or incompatible organisms.

Farmers have found that there are strict limits to the viability of selective breeding techniques which were originally designed to enhance features such as milk yields. Some mutations have been successful but they do not amount to much. All living creatures have within them hundreds or even thousands of genes which control and direct the functioning of their body parts. The genes act in a pre-determined sequence and, if any mutation is to succeed, the changes must be in place and properly connected. One can see that, if the continuing process of accommodating to any structural change is indeed happening all the time, then such a process would place a severe strain on the functionality and viability of existing genes and body structures, even allowing for the fact that evolution takes place gradually over thousands of generations.

Another problem with regard to Darwin's theory is the apparent paucity of fossils of intermediate animals, i.e., creatures which, within one single body structure, display features which originate from more than one species. Darwin acknowledged this problem but, it appears, there has been no breakthrough in trying to find an acceptable explanation for the almost total lack of visible and conclusive evidence of the theory of evolution. The millions of fossils excavated all over the world during the past few hundred years have not demonstrated evidence of "work-in-progress" in order to prove, beyond doubt, that a process of continuous morphing is taking place within all living organisms. There are precious few "transitional" creatures, i.e. creatures whose body parts were in various stages of evolving. According to the latest reports, even the fossil of the archaeopteryx does not show evidence of "half-finished" components or useless growths.

Of particular relevance to us, it is beyond dispute that there is a huge unbridged gap in the fossil record which purports to connect apes and humankind. As demonstrated in chapter 4, scientists have attempted to make a tenuous and understandable connection between the various hominids thought to be the precursors of *Homo sapiens*. I was careful to point out, however, that we cannot describe a direct connection between the species. And, in a direct challenge to Charles Darwin, many scientists have recently concluded that the 6 or 7 million years between *Toumai* and *H. sapiens* do not provide adequate time for the hominid species to have evolved as originally thought. Bearing in mind the very slow pace of micro-evolution, it is now considered physically impossible for the transformation to have taken place within that time-frame because the various amino acids and specialised proteins would not have had time to be created and to function properly.

Biologists love to demonstrate the Darwinian diagram which shows the alleged genetic inter-connectedness of all living things. But recent research has found that this theory is in need of some revision. Some scientists have asserted that it would be wrong to link microbes, fishes, plants and quadrupeds in a "tree-of-life" linear way. They say that each creature has exhibited features which have been wonderfully and uniquely designed.

For years evolutionists have triumphantly referred to the human appendix as a vestigial organ, proof that in the onward rush of evolution, nature has "forgotten" to eliminate any superfluous features from more primitive animals which would not be needed by *Homo sapiens*. However, the notion that the appendix is a useless organ is no longer valid because, (a) the appendix has been shown to provide safe housing for beneficial gut bacteria, and (b) numerous rodents and other primates have retained their appendix in spite of evolutionary pressures, indicating that, for many mammals, the appendix has always had a useful function.

Another question still to be answered by scientists is this: why have several species escaped from the clutches of the evolutionary process? Sponges, horse-shoe crabs, coelacanths and sea-cucumbers are just some of the species which have refused to march to the drum-beat of the evolutionary battalions, as envisioned by Darwin. Instead, their development seems to have remained stuck in a rut for hundreds of millions of years.

It is pertinent to report the result of a survey conducted in 2001 by the Discovery Institute, a think-tank in the USA, which leans towards the promotion of ideas relating to Intelligent Design. A total of some 800 highly trained biologists, physicists and anthropologists signed a "Dissent from Darwinism" statement, indicating that they were not completely happy with some of his ideas.

Irreducible Complexity

In his original theory of evolution Charles Darwin made the following claim:

> *"If it could be demonstrated that any complex organ existed, which could not possibly have been formed by numerous, successive, slight modifications, my theory would absolutely break down. But I can find no such cases."*

In recent years the scientific world has made great strides in developing and delving into the exciting new realm of nano-technology. One nanometre is one billionth of a metre. Being able to manipulate matter on such an atomic, molecular or supra-molecular scale can, potentially, lead to many benefits in medicine and industry. About 20 years ago researchers in the field of molecular biology discovered that, within each cell, there are complex miniature turbines generating energy. Tiny parts, made up of about 30 different proteins, resemble miniature rotors and drive shafts. Scientists have experimented with removing one or other proteins and they found that the motor function seizes up and will not function.

A leading biochemist, Dr. Michael Behe, has described the tiny motors operating in the biological world as "irreducibly complex". Let us use a familiar object to make the point. A simple camera, stripped down to its bare essentials, consists of a light-proof box, a lens, a shutter and a piece of photo-sensitive paper. If you remove any single one of these four parts it will not function as a camera. Likewise, in order to enable a bacterium to swim, it is necessary that it incorporates a *"bacterium flagellum"*, a short, whip-like appendage which the organism uses to propel itself around. It consists of a tiny rotor and other miniature components such as a propeller, a universal joint and a drive shaft. Dr. Behe has demonstrated that the flagellum is so perfectly structured that it ceases to function if any one part is missing. Crucially, the flagellum could not have been formed by gradual successive evolutionary changes. Because of its irreducible complexity the flagellum seems to suggest that Darwin's theory, which posits a slower evolutionary trajectory, is in need of qualification or amendment. At the very least, it creates some doubt and it raises the possibility of the existence of an evolutionary trajectory which is slightly different from that suggested by Darwin. It certainly raises the likelihood of an "assist" from someone or something.

The Quantum Revolution

For most of the past 400 years men of science have been wedded to the concept of "Determinism", the belief that major natural world events and the mind-set of living organisms are pre-ordained and their direction of travel is unalterable. In other words, said Sir Isaac Newton, we cannot escape from the rigidity of the classical natural laws of cause and effect.

The laws of physics, which were understood and developed by such great scientific luminaries as Newton and Einstein, propounded the idea that the world was made up of lumps of matter which behaved in accordance with laws of nature that are rigid and unshakable. Natural processes were thought to be constantly and smoothly moving along predetermined lines which were fairly predictable and they were not subject to interference from non-physical forces.

At one time or another, even non-physicists espoused the doctrine of determinism. Karl Marx believed that all the problems facing the world were due to the inherent and ever-present "evils of capitalism", rather than the unpredictable conscious day-to-day decisions taken by each of us in the world of our own free will. Likewise, Sigmund Freud, who also subscribed to the idea of determinism, believed that the world outlook of every person, together with any action he takes, are both the inevitable result of the workings of his inbuilt unconscious mind rather than by the exercise, on a daily basis, of the individual's free will.

Right up to the early part of the 20th century determinism held the attention of scientists, including Albert Einstein, who famously told a fellow-physicist, Niels Bohr, *"God does not play dice with the Universe."* Determinists perceived that the Universe functioned flawlessly and with incredible precision, with all systems working according to pre-determined factors caused by prior events that have occurred since the beginning of creation. Many freethinkers agreed with Laplace, Lamarck and Darwin that, in considering the creation of the Universe and the evolution of the species, God was an unnecessary and distracting hypothesis.

The person who demolished the case for determinism was Werner Carl Heisenberg. He worked on the "Quantum Revolution" theories of Max Planck. In 1900 the latter had discovered a now famous measure of energy. It is called "The Quantum," which posited the idea that energy flowed in "bits and pieces" rather than in a steady flow.

Heisenberg rattled the foundations of the laws of physics and it would be fair to say that his ideas have become very relevant in recent years. Quantum physics involves the study of the unseen sub-atomic world where nature is hesitant and uncertain. For example, if we were to try to measure the speed and the direction of travel of a particular electron, the very act of illuminating the electron sends out streams of light in the form of "chunks" and this immediately causes a radical change in the electron's behaviour. This means that it becomes impossible to measure both the electron's speed and its direction at any given moment. This inability has meant that, in the impossibly tiny world of the sub-atom, conditions are rather fuzzy, rather fluid, and very little is capable of precise measurement. This, in turn, means that there will always be an element of mystery in our Universe. Scientists will have to learn to work in a world which is unwilling to divulge all its secrets and where the rules governing the Universe cannot be described with absolute precision.

This theory has evoked a strong positive resonance among theists and others. It means that it would be wrong to look solely at the visible physical world in order to understand the ultimate processes of nature. Of course, test-tubes, precision scientific measuring instruments and mathematics have their place and their uses, but it would be too restraining and limiting if we did not look beyond the physical world in order to obtain a total picture of reality.

There is a "great ocean of truth" that remains to be discovered outside of physical reality, and scientists are now beginning to speak more openly about such matters as philosophy, conscious-ness and free will. The late Max Born, a Nobel Laureate in physics, even spoke of the developing tendency to take on board "something fixed ... (such as) ... God, beauty and truth."

It would be fair to say that, because of the introduction of the very powerful idea of "Indeterminism", as pioneered by Heisenberg, quantum physics has now turned the previously cosy materialist world upside down.

Because of the imprecision of nature it is now possible to introduce the concept of non-physical forces impinging upon and influencing physical reality. Some authoritative voices in the scientific world are warming to the idea that matter itself is just an alternative form of energy and, therefore, it does not consist solely of elementary particles as understood by classical physics. If we were to adopt this hypothesis it would be quite legitimate to say that belief in God is just as feasible as atheism. In other words, one cannot dismiss belief in a deity as totally invalid, and it has become perfectly acceptable to investigate religious concepts, in the same way as we have been used to investigating scientific theories.

Planck and Heisenberg have, in their own ways, given us the key to unlock a spiritual dimension of the world and they have exerted a powerful influence on sceptics who had previously been hesitant in exploring this aspect of reality.

What is Reality?

Naturally, all material things that we can see, touch, taste, smell and hear qualify as reality. But what can we say about human consciousness? The awareness of self is a phenomenon which is hard to explain but we can say that it is a peculiar and subjective dimension that all of us humans have within ourselves.

Scientists tell us that we are nothing more than a walking bundle of cells, energy, molecules and genes. But this does not explain how an organism such as ours can acquire the important faculty of self-awareness or consciousness. Furthermore, it provides no clue to explain how mankind was gifted with musical ability or artistic competence or the ability to conceptualise or derive meaning from patterns.

The neurons and synapses within our brains comprise the "hardware", so to speak, of our thought processes. But the mystery of consciousness is enshrined in the fact that this sophisticated hardware alone does not provide us with a faculty which is supra-physical.

Our five senses help us to understand and make sense of the world around us but these sensory perceptions are different as between one person and another. In a godless world our five senses would have been considered perfectly capable of revealing to us our own internal perception of the world around us. However, if two or more people are hearing a piece of music or admiring an impressive mountain view, we cannot say that they are all experiencing the same emotions or feelings. If each person in the group is reacting to a given phenomenon in a slightly different way then we cannot say that all perceptions have an independent, verifiable objective existence. Does that mean that images, consciousness, perceptions do not belong to the world of reality? Of course not. I believe that we need to make an effort to acknowledge and appreciate both physical reality and the many different manifestations of spiritual reality in order to fully understand both the "how" and the "why" of the world around us.

We all know what we mean when we say that we have experienced joy or sadness, love or fear. We all live with our hopes, feelings, imagination, dreams, ambitions, reflections. We have experienced all these things; they are real enough to each one of us, but they are not capable of being quantified, dissected and tested in a laboratory. Likewise, to a believer, the God hypothesis is as real as anything which we can experience through our five senses. We may not comprehend how or where or in what form God exists and we may be unsure how we should interact with Him. But intuitive faith, which is a faculty higher than intellect, teaches us that, to lead a truly functional and successful life, we need both our rational intellect and our spirituality. Each one of us humans, whether religious or not, we have within us an ideological proclivity, an aesthetic inclination which has very little to do with rationality. These tendencies inform our world-view and our perspective. It is therefore wrong for atheists to maintain that the millions of people all over the world who have maintained their faith are credulous simpletons, incapable of intellectual honesty.

The electrical pulses and the mechanical functions of even the most sophisticated computer cannot be said to have any concept of meaning and intention. A computer cannot be considered to possess a consciousness, even if it is loaded with masses of relevant software and even if it can perform mathematical calculations at a phenomenal speed or able to carry on a "conversation" with a human. The computer is not conscious of what it is doing, any more than the turntable on a record player can appreciate the finer points of a Beethoven symphony which it is reproducing.

If I were to place a lump of earth in one dish and the ground-up brain of Mozart in another dish, I would not be able to visually detect any essential difference, even though I were fully aware that the contents of the second dish belonged to somebody who had composed my favourite horn concerto. In other words, there must be something beyond the realm of the physical components of matter. One is led to the inevitable conclusion that consciousness, self-awareness and mind must have, at its origin, a non-worldly Power. A mere conjunction of chromosomes and gases cannot produce perceptions. Perception, ethics, morality, love, hope, empathy, altruism, all these faculties cannot be derived from the mere combination or fusion of molecules, chemicals, gases, cells, genes and DNA. There must be an over-arching Directing Mind.

The issue of consciousness is related to the equally mysterious reality of thought and the way we derive meaning from events occurring around us and beyond. Our human imagination enables us to devise patterns of thought that involve generalising and conceptualising. We can abstract and distinguish one set of patterns from another and we have the imagination to consider abstract concepts such as "democracy" and "freedom."

Although you use the brain hardware to deduce conclusions from a whole series of facts and situations, it is not your brain that makes the ultimate decision or conclusion as to how to react or take action – that decision emanates from the collective or whole "you."

I like the idea, suggested some time ago by the physicist Sir Arthur Eddington, that our journey through life can be likened to our taking a stroll along the sea-shore. As we breathe in the fresh air, as we pick up a smooth pebble or a pretty seashell and admire its shape and striations of colour, we should keep in mind that, hidden under the waves, there could be unseen treasures waiting to be discovered. Reality, therefore, is not only about the physical things we can see, touch, hear, taste and smell. It follows that we could enrich our lives by opening our minds to the existence of an unseen deity. Failure to embrace that possibility might result in our missing out on something valuable and potentially life-enhancing.

Today, none of us can say that we have seen God, but, like a field of sunflowers with their heads turned towards the sun, most of us look up to the heavens and we do believe, to a lesser or greater extent, that God is there somewhere. Countless people, all over the world, find that knowledge comforting and supportive. In times of personal or national danger, or if we are about to undertake an important or life-changing enterprise, we turn to silent prayer. We do it because it works. It is therapy which both calms us and emboldens us to strive and to achieve the physically impossible.

SCIENTIFIC TERMS
EXPLAINED

(My thanks are due to Dr. Leslie Savoy for his valuable advice in ensuring the accuracy of the following definitions):

An **ATOM** is the smallest possible unit of any element. The term is derived from a Greek word meaning uncuttable or indivisible. An atom represents energy moving so fast in a circle that it appears and functions as something solid, but all atoms are more than 99% devoid of matter and consist of blank, empty space. An atom possesses no life and can only be viewed individually using special equipment. Even a tiny dust mite contains millions of atoms. The composition of an atom can be compared to a tiny solar system. There is a nucleus which contains the bulk of the material (protons and neutrons) and there are very tiny electrons whizzing around in orbit around the nucleus. It is now known that protons and neutrons are made up of even smaller sub-atomic particles – fermions, quarks, and the Higgs boson.

THE STORY OF HUMANKIND

A total of 118 different kinds of atoms have been identified so far. They are technically called **CHEMICAL ELEMENTS**, of which 98 occur naturally, and the rest have been created by scientists. Examples of elements include gold, mercury and oxygen. Elements are listed according to their atomic number on the periodic table, which, in turn, refers to the number of protons in their nucleus.

If two or more different elements are combined you get a **COMPOUND**. Water is a compound because it consists of two atoms of hydrogen plus one atom of oxygen.

A MOLECULE is a group of two or more atoms bonded together chemically. A water molecule has three atoms: two atoms of hydrogen and one of oxygen. Other molecules may comprise hundreds of atoms. All compounds are molecules but not all molecules are compounds.

A CELL is the basic unit of life. It is the smallest thing that can be considered a living thing. There are approximately 50 trillion cells in a human body, whereas bacteria and amoebas are examples of life contained in a single cell. Inside every cell there are four macromolecules (i.e. very large molecules) which are the building blocks of life. These macromolecules comprise Proteins (chains of amino acids), Nucleic Acids (mainly DNA), Carbohydrates and Lipids (fats and oils).

Cells divide constantly and naturally, although unrestrained cell division can lead to tumours or cancers. Many human cells can reproduce their entire genome (i.e. the entire set of genetic instructions) in a cyclic event taking about 24 hours.

PROTEINS are the building blocks of body tissue. They are made up of a chain of several different amino acids, each having unique individual formulae. The actual order of amino acids in any protein chain is specific to that protein but may vary slightly from species to species, and this is genetically determined.

Proteins play a vital role in every living organism, responsible for performing a huge range of different bodily tasks – powering muscles, controlling the speed of chemical reactions and attacking invading bacteria. For example, haemoglobin is a protein found in red blood cells. When coupled to iron it enables the transport of oxygen throughout the body. Aside from water, proteins form the most abundant substance in the human body and, when combined with DNA, they carry genetic information from parent to progeny.

DNA is an acid macromolecule which is found in all living organisms and which, when combined with proteins, forms a chromosome that carries the genetic code. It can reproduce itself with the aid of specific enzymes. In 1953 Crick and Watson announced their groundbreaking discovery of the molecular structure of DNA, which has the form of a twisted ladder, a double helix, where each of the two strands is complementary to the other. The rungs of the ladder are made up of base pairs of four nucleotides, A, C, G and T, while the outside structure is made up of alternating phosphates and a unique sugar, deoxyribose. These four nucleotides (adenine, cytosine, guanine and thymine respectively) control all the relevant functions of a cell and they are set out in sequence – in the same way as a bar-code on a food packet purchased in a supermarket. When they are attached together the resultant string represents the DNA of that organism.

Even a tiny virus or a single-cell organism (e.g. bacteria) can contain more than 5,000 nucleotides, while other living organisms could have several hundred thousand or several million or even billions of nucleotides in a long chain.

DNA is one of the two constituent parts of a chromosome, the other part being a group of specific proteins called histones. DNA is found tightly coiled surrounding protein material. The reason for the tight coil is that DNA may consist of thousands or even millions of the aforementioned nucleotides. In fact, if the DNA molecules in a single human cell could be unwound and placed end-to-end, the string would extend to over 1 metre (about 4 ft.) in length. What unites all of biology is the fact that the same nucleotides form the fundamental information system that first evolved more than 3.5 billion years ago and is found in all living organisms. Although a human being looks totally different from, say, a lump of yeast, yet at the genetic level all the genes are made up of the same substance, DNA, and for any particular gene the base sequence is more or less the same. This indicates that evolution is tremendously conservative and economical.

The letters of the genetic code, i.e. the nucleotides A, C, G, and T, are translated into protein through the means of something called RNA (ribonucleic acid), whose principal role is to act as a messenger, carrying instructions from DNA in order to create the vitally important proteins. Now that the genetic code and the mechanism by which it is decoded by cells is known by science, a whole new medical vista has been opened up – many medical laboratories are attempting the manipulation of DNA in the pursuit of finding cures for a variety of diseases.

CHROMOSOMES are found in the nucleus of every cell. They consist of thread-like molecules, a combination of DNA and protein. When combined, they are collected into units called genes. Each chromosome is a package that holds several genes – a set of instructions that make up who we are.

Each species has a characteristic number of chromosomes. It was not until 1956 that scientists established beyond doubt that there are 23 pairs of chromosomes in every human cell, 22 pairs of which look the same in both males and females, while the 23rd pair is the sex chromosome, which differs in that females have two copies of the "X" chromosome while males have one "X" and one "Y" chromosome. By way of contrast, dogs have 39 pairs of chromosomes, while fruit flies have just 4 pairs.

GENES, found in the cells of all living organisms, code for different characteristics – e.g. hair colour, or the shape of a horse's head, or the structure of an eagle's wings or the scent of a rose – which are transmitted from one generation to the next. Genes occupy a fixed position on a chromosome. Within the human body there are about 30,000 to 35,000 genes. By contrast, a simple bacterium may contain as few as 500 genes. Genes are capable of replication and recombination and, of course, they can mutate, sometimes resulting in sickness such as cancer.

Genes act as templates for making proteins, the vital material responsible for performing a huge range of different bodily tasks. Your genes are unique to you – unless you have an identical twin brother or sister. Slightly more than half your genes are inherited from your mother and the rest from your father. The genetic code (i.e. the succession of letters in a genome sequence) is universal for all species but there are some distinct variations in the genes of different species and even between different individuals of the same species.

Genes can be turned on and off. This process occurs naturally and is crucial in distinguishing and separating those cells which, for example, will eventually go on to become a human liver from the cells which will ultimately go on to form, say, an eye or a hand. Genes act in concert with one another. In other words, every living organism can be viewed as a co-operative bundle of genes.

The word **GENOME** is used to refer to all of the genes, comprising all of the DNA in an organism – the whole set of genetic instructions. The human genome contains six billion letters or nucleotides (A, C, G and T), approximately three billion letters of which are inherited from your mother and three billion from your father.

In 1990 scientists in USA started the Human Genome Project, under the direction of Dr. Francis Collins. It was a vast collaborative international attempt at decoding all the human body's genetic information. In effect, it was an attempt to locate every human gene and read its instruction manual in detail. The first stage of the project was completed in 2000 and cost more than £2 billion. Since then numerous genome sequences have been produced, both of human and animal species as well as bacteria. It is now possible to produce, on demand, an individual person's distinctive genome sequence at a cost of less than £1,000.

CARBON is a chemical element which has been known since antiquity. It is one of the most common elements in the Earth's crust, the fourth most abundant element in the Universe by mass, after hydrogen, helium and oxygen. Carbon forms the chemical basis of all known life on Earth and is found in abundance in the sun, the stars, the comets and the atmosphere of most planets. When combined with oxygen and hydrogen it can form many groups of compounds, such as sugars, fats and alcohol. There are three types of carbon (called isotopes), carbon 12, carbon 13 and carbon 14. The latter is used to date early fossils.

HYDROGEN was discovered following the work of Robert Boyle, Henry Cavendish and Antoine Lavoisier in the eighteenth century. The atomic number of hydrogen is 1 as its nucleus contains only one proton. Hydrogen and helium are by far the most abundant elements in the Universe.

OXYGEN is colourless, odourless and tasteless and is the third most abundant element in the Universe. Oxygen makes up approximately 65% of the human body.

DEUTERIUM, also known as heavy hydrogen, is naturally abundant on planet Earth, both in the atmosphere and in the oceans. It is found everywhere in the ratio of 156 atoms of deuterium to 1 million atoms of hydrogen. It is an essential element in the formation of helium. Nearly all the deuterium on Earth was produced during the process of fusion which took place 13.8 billion years ago, when the Universe was created as a result of the "Big Bang." Deuterium is thought to have played a big part in setting the number and ratio of the various chemical elements existing on planet Earth today. The abundance of deuterium has been proved to have remained remarkably constant over billions of years and this fact appears to lend credence to the theory that the creation of the Universe was a single momentous event, rather than the result of a series of multiple events occurring at different times.

There are many uses of deuterium in organic chemistry and it is an essential element in producing "Heavy Water" in the nuclear fission reactors, where it takes the place of water. Of course, it will play a crucial role as and when commercial fusion becomes an accomplished technology.

INDEX

justice, pursuit of, 126

Kepler, Johannes, 18
Kierkegaard, Soren, 115

lamprey, 58
lancelet, 56
language, evolution of, 73, 74
Large Hadron Collider, 21
Lemaître, Georges, 18
Lennox, Prof. John, 13
lev, 96
life, commencement of, 27
Linnaeus, Carl, 40
living organism "kingdoms":
  primitive classification, 55
  modern classification, 40
"Lucy":
  Australopithecus Afarensis, 66

macro and micro evolution, 198
Maimonides, Moses:
  105, 119, 144, 149
major plant species and trees:
  decomposition, 58
Malala Yousafzai, 151
Mammals:
  development, 61
  number of species, 64
mammoths, extinction, 61
Marx, Karl, 176, 204
Milky Way Galaxy, 23
Miller-Urey experiment, 34
miracles, attitude towards, 120
mitzvoth, 96, 113
modern humankind:
  ancient belief in spirits, 79
  created in image of God, 95
  relationship to God, 112

triumph of, 75
moon, creation of, 26, 32
moral values, evolution, 138
morality:
  "acceptable" behaviour, 128
  sources and origin, 128
  "what ought to be", 130
Moses, 93, 100, 110, 129, 138
multiverse, 28
Muslims, treatment of Jews, 135
Mutation, natural selection, 35, 38

na'asei ve-nishma'a, 98
natural catastrophes, 158
nefesh, 95
neshamah 96, 109
Newton, Sir Isaac, 18
Noachide laws, 80
nuclear fusion, 23
nucleotides, 213, 214

"On the Origin of Species", 35
Ordovician Period, 57
origin of life, 193
oxygen, 35, 56, 217

pain and suffering:
  theistic response, 160
paintings/etchings on cave walls:
  77, 123, 169
Palmyra, 137
Pascal, Blaise, 185
Pasternak, Boris, 155
Pasteur, Louis, 194
Patterson, Dr. Colin, 45
Penzias, Arno, 20, 188
Perimeter Institute, 28
Permian Period, 58